ROD WO

President of Four Grainer LLC, jewelry business consultant, and host of "Inside the Jewelry Trade" radio show.

Rod has 25+ years of growing jewelry stores into profitable businesses. Are you next?

He is the author of *Chant to Be Heard* and *Power Chant for Success*.

Contact Rod at FourGrainer.com or directly at Rod@FourGrainer.com.

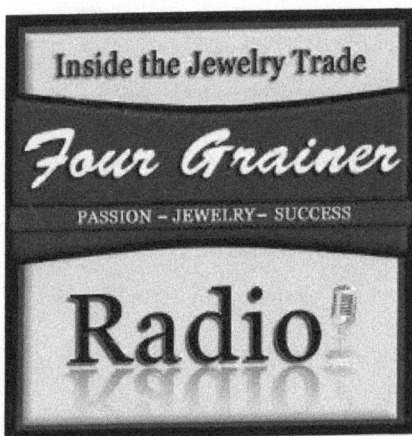

THE JEWELRY TRADE RADIO SHOW

The premier on-demand internet radio program for the jewelry trade.

Never miss an episode! Download our free app for your mobile phone or tablet.

A Reason to Chant: How to Take Control of Your Marketing to Earn Trust, Devotion and Traffic for your Brand Forever,
by Rod Worley

Book design by Adam Robinson for GoodBookDevelopers.com

Published by Four Grainer LLC
1911 Grayson Hwy
Ste 8 - 330
Grayson, GA 30017

www.fourgrainer.com

Four Grainer
PASSION – JEWELRY– SUCCESS

A Reason to Chant

How to Take Control of Your Marketing to Earn

- ✓ Trust,
- ✓ Devotion,
- ✓ and Traffic

for Your Brand *Forever*

Rod Worley

FourGrainer LLC

Atlanta, Georgia

"Do not follow where the path may lead. Go instead where there is no path and leave a trail."

—Ralph Waldo Emerson

CONTENTS

HOW TO READ THIS BOOK   1

CHAPTER ONE   3
A Frozen Stadium Seat in Cleveland

CHAPTER TWO   9
Can You Hear Me Now?

CHAPTER THREE   26
A Disruptive, Clean-Sheet Approach to Marketing

CHAPTER FOUR   31
What Exactly Is Actively Involved Marketing?

CHAPTER FIVE   43
*A Fly On the Wall—What Clients & Staff Say
About the Program*

CHAPTER SIX   54
The NFL vs. Charities—Not Even Close

CHAPTER SEVEN   59
Physically Setting Up The A.I.M. Program

CHAPTER EIGHT   82
Setting the Record Straight About Marketing & ROI

CHAPTER NINE   97
How Much Do You Donate Per Person?

CHAPTER TEN   120
Fears, Tears, And Launching the Right Way

WHAT'S UP NEXT?   131

To Cynthia my love, for nearly three decades you've encouraged me to dream, to take chances, to explore beyond the horizon.

All is possible with you in my life.

HOW TO READ THIS BOOK

"One's mind, once stretched by a new idea,
never regains its original dimensions."
—Oliver Wendell Holmes Sr.

THIS BOOK IS A STEP BY STEP GUIDE OF how to take control of your marketing to earn trust, devotion and traffic to your brand forever.

It's not a book of esoteric marketing theories, high brow advertising musings, or fancy charts in multiple colors.

It's written so you can hand this book to your summer intern in the morning and by that afternoon they've read it, have a clear understanding of the program, and know how to get it set up and running.

This book delivers the proven results of the Four Grainer "Actively Involved Marketing" (A.I.M.) program in the following areas:

- First and foremost, this program drives traffic to your brick and mortar store.
- It brings in people who've never visited your store.
- Compels former clients and your current customer base to revisit your store.

- Grants you complete control over every aspect of this marketing program.
- Ensures that costs, results and profit are 100% measurable.
- Delivers your brand message to the community the right way.
- Provides the name, address, telephone number and email address of everyone this program brings to your store.
- Creates content that engages and grows your social media platforms organically.
- Costs less than $20 to set up and only pennies every year to maintain.
- Gives the local community a real reason to chant your business's name!

The results I'm going to share are the culmination of two years of actually running the Four Grainer program in a brick and mortar store.

We've witnessed first hand increased profitability, seen how it's transformed the client's image of the store, seen authentic one-on-one bonds created, and seen how it's positively impacted every aspect of their marketing.

These proven results will work in ANY business wishing to increase the number of clients walking through the door.

Accounting firms, car dealerships, dentists, law firms, jewelry stores, restaurants—any business, no matter how large or small—can benefit from using these proven strategies.

Enjoy!

Chapter One

A FROZEN STADIUM
SEAT IN CLEVELAND

*"It was so bitterly cold outside that by the time
I walked back to the car, the footlong sand-
wich I got at Subway shrunk to a 6 inch"*
—A Modern Witticism

T O SAY IT WAS COLD THAT DAY WOULD BE
an understatement.

It was the kind of cold that settles down deep inside
your body and stays with you hours after you finally find
warmth.

The kind of cold that robs you of precious body heat
with every single breath.

You seriously wonder why anyone in their right
mind would be sitting on frozen plastic stadium seats,
surrounded by a foot of hard packed snow. But there
you sat with your Pittsburgh friends in an open-air NFL
football stadium in Cleveland, Ohio in January.

In the end, win or lose it's just one of the perks of being
a lifelong Pittsburgh Steeler fan.

You've lost track of the hundreds of dollars you've paid for tickets, transportation and the many Steelers products you wear with pride. All this for the privilege to visit exotic, far-flung tourist destinations such as Cleveland and Cincinnati in the dead of a face-freezing January winter.

Honestly, in spite of this, you wouldn't miss a game for the world because there's a visceral feeling of belonging, of being a part of the cause—a Steeler Nation if you will—that feeds something primordial inside of you.

You're there to experience the moment, to cheer as the team takes the field, and when it's all on the line in a game, the crowd collectively rises to their feet.

Nothing quite like it, thousands of people on their feet, so passionate about the outcome that their greatest outpouring of genuine support and solidarity is to chant, "*Dee*—fence" or "Here we go Steelers, here we go!"

That's when it hits you.

The Pittsburgh Steelers are a brand, a business striving to establish their brand identity just like every other business.

A successful brand for sure—their six Super Bowl trophies are evidence of that—but still just another business.

Genuine fan fanaticism aside, they provide goods and services just like your business does, except for one significant difference.

They give their fans a reason to chant!

***

We know what you're thinking, and you're right.

This book is about how to earn trust and devotion to your small business and not about freezing your backside off at an NFL football game. The reason for the NFL example is because they've made a genuine multi-generational connection which resonates with their fans, or for the purposes of this discussion, their "clients."

They've found the touch points that moves their fans to purchase goods and services at the rate of $12 billion a year.

This book is going to reveal how to make a connection in your local community, how to make your clients more passionate and more deeply-rooted, just as you see displayed for the NFL on Sunday.

In today's business environment it isn't enough that everyone knows your company's name.

To grow your market share today, you have to stand out in a virtual sea of advertising.

To truly be elite, you have to give your clients a reason to chant your name.

***

So how do we get your brick and mortar business from where you are now, to where you know you really should be?

First, we're going to pull back the curtain and expose the dirty little secrets about the ineffectiveness of your current marketing efforts.

Next, we'll take you step-by-step through a proven clean-sheet "disruptive" approach to marketing which finally puts you in total control of your marketing success.

Here are the results we're going to deliver:

- First and foremost, drive foot traffic to your store.
- Get your real brand message out to the community.
- Give you a marketing program where the cost, results, and profit are 100% measurable.
- Hand you the name, address, telephone number, and email address of everyone the program brings to your store.
- Provide content that engages and grows your social media platforms organically.
- Cost less than $20 initially to set up and only pennies every year to maintain.
- Build trust, loyalty, and devotion to your brand.

***

We know it's a lot to promise and to be quite honest, we live in an age where so many over promise and woefully under deliver. Fortunately, that's not the case here.

This book details two years of using the Four Grainer "Actively Involved Marketing" program in a small business and seeing the actual results first hand.

The marketing program was born out of the necessity to reach the full range of consumers.

We define a full range of consumers as:

- Potential new clients who've never been to your store.
- Former customers who haven't been to your store in over a year.

- Clients who've shopped in your store within the current year.

We can all agree that your business needs fans as passionate as NFL fans but ...

Here's the first problem: you're not the multi-billion dollar NFL, but you need a devoted fan base, and you need to have your brand message clearly heard and understood.

You need to differentiate your brand from your competitors, but you don't have a billion dollar marketing budget like the NFL to throw at the problem, nor do you have a team of elite marketers handling every nuance of your advertising message on a 24/7 basis.

In many small businesses, it's typically the owner, or at most a team of two or three that handle everything.

Unfortunately, there's an even bigger problem: your marketing efforts are facing shortcomings and limitations, and you probably don't know what they are.

These deficiencies are often actually costing you tens of thousands of valuable marketing dollars while giving you a false sense of hope that you're reaching your local community.

Let's be honest, the people in your local community are the very ones you MUST reach for your business to thrive and grow.

Nobody wants to talk about it, and certainly, nobody wants to take the time to research the formidable marketing challenges facing small businesses in today's hyper-crowded rich-media world.

John Wanamaker famously said in the early 1900s, "Half the money I spend on advertising is wasted; the trouble is I don't know which half."

Instinctively John Wanamaker was right back then, and deep inside you feel the same way about your advertising today.

After this next chapter, you're going to have a clear view of which half of your marketing dollars you are throwing out the window.

We've done the research and we'll share it with you, so you can drill down and get the documented facts that the sellers of advertising don't want you to know.

They say that knowledge is power, so get ready to become very powerful indeed!

Chapter Two

CAN YOU HEAR ME NOW?

"The single biggest problem with communication is the illusion that it has taken place"
—James Bernard Shaw

YOU MAY NOT KNOW HIS NAME, BUT PAUL Marcarelli has summed up your business marketing problems in these five words, "Can You Hear Me Now?"

You'd certainly recognize Paul Marcarelli if you saw his face. From 2002 to 2011 he was the American actor who played the ubiquitous "Test Man" character in the commercial series ("Can you hear me now?") for Verizon Wireless. He appeared in all of his Verizon advertisements wearing a gray Verizon jacket and his horn-rimmed glasses.

Paul tells you it's never been easier to communicate your thoughts and ideas with others around the planet than it is right now, and he is 100% correct. The problem is everyone's talking at once, and no one is listening.

A single voice.

Your business voice.

Is never getting heard.

Surprisingly it's the same challenges facing Fox News, Apple, the American Red Cross, and the local accountant down the street.

And that is?

Your business, every news outlet, entertainment platform, and cute cat video on YouTube are fighting it out every day for attention in a very crowded space.

How crowded?

On average, people spend more than 490 minutes of their day (8.16 hours) with some form of media, this according to a new report by ZenithOptimedia published on May 31st, 2015 in an article titled, "Internet use to drive 1.4% increase in media consumption in 2015."

Television remains dominant, accounting for three hours of daily use—which is an hour more than the second place Internet browsing.

The report measured the media consumed in its traditional form—for example, a broadcast viewed on television (cable, satellite) or printed newspapers being physically read.

Watching videos on the web or reading a newspaper's website counts as Internet consumption.

By the way, good luck with the advertisement you placed in the local print newspaper.

When compared to 2010, here's the change in daily media consumption by medium as reported by ZenithOptimedia:

- Internet—Consumption up by 105% since 2010
- Outdoor signage—Up 3%
- Television—Down 8%

- Cinema—Down 11%
- Radio—Down 15%
- Magazines—Down 23%
- Newspapers—Down 31%

By 2017, studies have estimated we'll find even more time in our day to take in media. Apparently, half of our waking life is not enough.

According to ZenithOptimedia, the average global consumption is expected to rise to 506 minutes per day (8.43 hours).

In the Media Dynamic article titled, "Adults Spend Almost 10 Hours Per Day With The Media, But Note Only 150 Ads" dated September 9th, 2014, they showed commercial clutter on TV has increased steadily.

However, viewers today have options to avoid commercials. Remote controls, DVR's and a wider variety of channels to choose from enable viewers to skip commercials. Many households are "cutting the cord" and switching to alternative ways of viewing programs commercial free.

Nevertheless, the average person, the study points out, is bombarded by the cumulative effect of 360 ads per day across five different media sources: TV, radio, internet, newspapers and magazines.

Of these 360, only 150 to 155 are even consciously noted. When you dig deeper, you'll find that out of the 150 to 155 ads noticed in a single day that few have a strong enough impact to be recalled later.

If you can't remember the ad, how can it make an impression that ultimately leads to a sale?

Apparently, we're consuming more media than ever which makes it much tougher for your ads to make an impact with your audience.

Fortunately, we still have the tried and true, print newspaper to fall back on. The newspaper has always been the Rock of Gibraltar for brick and mortar stores. Since time immemorial, print and its ever growing subscriber base have always been consistent.

So how is the tried and true printed newspaper holding up in today's digital age? Well, not so good, it seems. The U.S. print newspaper business is on life support.

Let's start with these numbers from the Newspaper Association of America as reported in the "State of the News Media 2015," published on April 29th, 2015 by the Pew Research Center. According to the report, print ad revenues have fallen from $44.9 billion in 2003 to just $16.4 billion in 2014. Conversely, digital ad revenues have been steady at $3.5 billion since 2006.

Circulation for the print newspaper is falling like a rock.

The major print newspapers took a deep plunge in subscribers between 2013 and 2015. Consider the circulation numbers for these major print platforms.

- The Wall Street Journal is down 400,000 subscribers.
- NY Times has dropped 200,000 subscribers.
- The Washington Post is down 100,000.

- The Los Angeles Times has lost 100,000 in annual subscribers.

The fact is, according to Dan Kennedy in his article "Print Is Dying, and Digital Is No Savior: The Long, Ugly Decline Of The Newspaper Business Continues Apace" (dated January 2016), the Internet option certainly isn't saving those print newspapers. The article ends with this summary, "For the beleaguered newspaper business, the walls are closing in, and the oxygen is being pumped out of the room."

Well, at least we still have television to get the word out, or do we?

Tough Times for TV Advertisers

Since 1941, televisions has been used as an advertising medium. With all of its distinct advantages, several recent studies have concluded that the amount of time watching traditional TV is dropping for every adult age group.

Not surprisingly an eMarketer study dated April 14, 2016, stated, "Americans between the ages 18 to 24 watch the least amount of traditional TV." This age group also dropped the fastest when compared to the other age groups, and they are clearly going elsewhere for their content. This year, the 18 to 24 age group will consume just over 2 hours and 22 minutes of traditional TV. That's in sharp contrast to the 6 hours and 3 minutes of viewing for those 65 and over.

Let's not kid ourselves either. In today's world, the financial cost to run the sheer number of TV ads needed to drive people into your store is out of the reach of most brick and mortar businesses.

Here are just a few of the expenses.

Five Financial Concerns with an Ad Campaign on TV:

- Point One—Total overall cost. When you consider the cost of production and distribution, few advertising mediums can eat up your budget as quickly at TV.
- Point Two—Production cost. The higher the production quality, the more it will cost for the various factors such as hiring script writers, producers, actors, film editors. You get what you pay for, and it shows.
- Point Three—Getting seen. After the commercial is ready, you'll still have to pay for air time. Since studies have shown that TV ads are the most effective with repetition, you'll need to purchase entire blocks of air time.
- Point Four—Change costs. It's costly to make changes because it means updating your script and reshooting the entire ad in many cases.
- Point Five—Hitting a moving target. With all of the research on viewership at your fingertips, it can still be tough to target your core audience effectively.

Remember that it isn't enough for people to simply see your ad, they have to take action because of it.

In a report published by Rutgers Business School, "11 Studies Prove Digital Marketing ROI" dated Friday,

December 19th, 2014, showed that according to Nielsen, traditional advertisers in the fast moving consumer goods section (F.M.C.G.) of business face a problem.

While the companies are allocating 60% of their media budget to television, the study showed only 18% of TV advertising campaigns generate a positive ROI (Return On Investment).

So what's the answer?

Where's everyone headed to get their message heard since traditional marketing is dropping in readership, viewership, and prominence?

The Internet Will Save Advertising!

I remember the articles like it was yesterday. The splashy banner style headlines like, "Print is Dead, Long Live The Internet!" or the numerous articles over the past few years about the potential for explosive advertising growth on mobile devices.

There's something inside our optimistic human nature which leads us to believe technology will somehow come to our aid on how to get our message out to the masses.

So much so that an article dated March 11th, 2016 in MediaLife titled, "As Digital Advertising Grows, So Do Questions," by Bill Cromwell posed the question "Does online advertising work?" It went on to ask, "Does it work so well that it deserves to siphon off large portions of your ad dollars from your other media?"

Many businesses are embracing the digital option for spreading their brand message because they see their costs rise and the effectiveness diminished in traditional marketing (TV, radio, magazine, and newspaper).

However, digital marketing, for all of its inherent advantages, has some real problems itself. At the top of the list has to be click fraud.

What's click fraud you ask?

Click fraud is an illegal practice happening when individuals or automated computer programs called "bots" (short for robot) click on a website's click-through advertisements.

This click-through can either be banner ads or paid text links to increase the numbers of clicks payable to the advertiser.

These automated computer "bot" programs are designed to seek out and interact with your particular display ads. Bot creators have monetized the process to bring them a sizable profit at the expense of advertisers. Marketers are then left paying for thousands of impressions that were never actually seen by real people.

The bill stacks up to a staggering amount across the globe, this according to Marketing Land in their January 19th, 2016 article by Greg Sterling titled, "Study: Sophisticated Bots Outwitting Marketers, Will Cost $7.2 Billion In 2016."

Online marketers have an easy time selling ad space by saying, "We can track your advertising investment." Here's the problem, though: few people understand the true definition of an "impression" in the digital world.

Most small businesses think that it refers to one "human being" seeing your ad once. Au contraire.

The truth is, and what sellers of online advertising never get around to telling you is that it just means one web browser is making a single digital request for an advertisement from your ad network.

Even though a human never saw your ad, even though a programmed computer bot has accessed it, you still pay.

Why should you care?

Multiple studies have shown that 60% of Internet traffic is computer bot traffic. Each time a malicious bot loads a web page, the browser makes a request to your ad network to load your advertisement. That action by the bot counts as a paid-for impression, even though no human being will see it.

Hold on. It gets much worse.

In the article titled, "The Definition Of An Ad Impression" by Reid Tatoris, February 18, 2014, in the Marketing Daily, "Only 8% of impressions have the opportunity to be seen by a real person." Reid went on to say, "Let me clarify: that does not mean that 8% of impressions are seen. That means only 8% have the chance to be seen."

Not good odds, not even by Las Vegas standards.

What good are the numbers if they are entirely skewed—made worthless—by click fraud, and you're left paying the bill?

What about mobile digital ads?

The news isn't good there either.

Author Kevin Lee in his article titled "Measurement and Attribution Top Challenges for Getting Mobile

Right" published on December 2nd, 2015 in ClickZ wrote, that overwhelmingly, the largest problem they had with mobile display advertising is determining if it was effective in bringing in business.

The ironic fact in all of this is these are the same people who are considered experts in mobile marketing and even they can't figure out if it is effective!

Wait, did someone mention ad blockers?

Ad blocking is a problem that none of the sellers of online advertisement want to talk about with prospective clients.

The March 11th, 2016 Smashing Magazine article by Vitaly Friedman titled, "A Never-Ending Story On Ad-Blockers" stated that "ad-blocker usage has grown from 12% in 2012 to 55% today."

For many online users, banner ads are mechanically blocked by a user installed program, or we've just tuned them out because we know they're just advertising.

According to a Goo study titled: "Most of Us Ignore Online Ads" dated February 2014, four out of five American consumers ignore online ads.

The result of these research points is a legitimate concern for advertisers today.

The problem is online ads have become so pervasive that many say they are now tuning them out altogether. In fact, a recent study by Google itself showed that 69% of web users left a site when an interruptive display ad popped up.

Any other ways clients block your advertisements?

For that answer, we turn to Mimi An in her article titled, "Native Advertising Rises As Consumers Opt Out" published on February 8th, 2016 for HubSpot.

According to the HubSpot's Global Interruptive Ads Survey:

- 94% of all consumers skip television ads entirely.
- 94% unsubscribe from email.
- 27% toss out direct mail before reading it.
- 50% of all shoppers are on the national "Do Not Call" registry.

What is the average brick and mortar business to do? Where can they turn? Is there anything that technology can give us to spread our message across the globe for free?

Social Media to the Rescue!

We've basked in the soft glow and hype about social media for the past ten years or so. The success stories can quickly fill you with wide-eyed wonder at the possibilities. Unlike other marketing platforms, social media is a two-edged sword.

There are some tremendous upsides to putting together a coordinated social media marketing initiative with your traditional marketing: it can reach an incredibly huge audience, it's a fast way to get your message out, and when done right, can nurture brand loyalty. Another real upside is that the major social media platforms are free to join.

The downside is that you quickly incur charges both in sponsored posts, content creation, and a paid community manager if you intend to make a real impact.

The dark side of social media marketing is that if you have a bad reputation for inferior products or services, the only thing these various free platforms will do is get that message out to the public faster and further. Social media has other limitations as well.

The Four Biggest Pitfalls of Social Media

Pitfall #1: Time-consuming

64% of digital marketers spend six hours or more on these sites.

Do you have that much extra time in your already busy day?

Pitfall #2: Generates negative troll users

Some people just want to cause problems from the deep, dark safety of their Mother's basement. These social trolls seem bent on causing as much havoc as possible with their vile, hateful postings. Eventually, every online brand must face them, the more popular you are, the more you'll probably have.

Pitfall #3: Your content being "scraped"

Once you post content, you run the risk of it being copied and used by others for their purposes. It's called "scraping," and it uses Internet bots to gather data from your site to post on their website and their other online platforms.

They also use it to undercut your promotional pricing, steal leads, and hijack marketing campaigns.

Pitfall #4: Social media marketing ROI is hard to define

As you read the various articles, white papers, and conference recaps, most digital marketers seem to have the same burning question you do. "How can you accurately measure the Return On Investment of their social media efforts?"

It's true. Most sellers of social media cannot give you a hard and fast ROI for their "must-have" apps and programs. The best they can usually do, when pressed on the topic, is to roll out one of these Mark Twain-like sayings such as, "The ROI of social media is that your business will still be around in five years," or, "Saying Hello to your clients doesn't have an ROI. It's about building relationships."

This next one is easily one of our personal favorites when these vendors call us: "What's the ROI of putting your pants on every day? It's hard to measure, but there are adverse consequences for not doing it."

Seriously? That's the best answer the "experts" can come up with to your question?

Bottom line here is that if you can't determine the return on investment of social media, how does your business gauge if you should spend more on a platform or cut it out altogether? All of that leads us to our favorite myths about the various social platforms. Are you sitting down?

According to a Custora research report conducted during the first quarter of 2014, "Social tactics are not meaningful sales drivers." The results appeared in an article on Media Post dated May 20th, 2014 by Erik Sass with the ominous title, "Social Media Accounts For Only 1% Of Online Retail Sales."

Custora looked at purchases from retail websites in the first quarter of the year to determine where the orders originated. And yes, the title of the article said it all. Less than 1% of those purchases originated from social media.

When it comes to social media being a driver of sales, most businesses clearly have the wrong impression. Most are convinced the number of "Followers" of your brand page equals the number of potential sales. The truth is social media does assist in the selling process, but seldom does it translate directly into a sale.

What usually happens instead is that social media assists conversions through helping people find out about your brand, and building trust and engagement before the consumer makes the actual purchase. It may take days, even weeks, before your customer returns to your website or physical store to make a purchase. Many brick and mortar stores, meanwhile, lose interest in managing their social platforms within three months. Abandoned social media sites, from every corner of the business world, litter the Internet.

Before we move on, we've got one more point to make on this subject.

Last Word On Social Media for Your Business

Social media started out as an innovative way to easily connect with family and friends while living a hectic lifestyle.

By its very name, it was created to be social in nature.

When social media exploded in popularity around 2010, businesses saw a free, easy way to blast their message into the stratosphere.

Looking back, you honestly couldn't help but stare in wide-eyed amazement at the potential to reach billions of people around the world with your brand message.

Business took what had worked for 100 years in traditional print marketing and tried to force it to work in social media.

Yes, there were some early successes, stories that have now risen to the level of urban legends where neighborhood brick and mortar stores were selling big ticket items to a client halfway around the world.

Somewhere along the way, though, businesses forgot that social media platforms were created originally to be social, not business related. People were there to socialize, not to be fed a steady stream of banner ads and interrupted at every turn with brand messages.

Today consumers primarily use social media for connection and entertainment. If your message doesn't fulfill one of those two requirements, chances are you're wasting your time, money and finger strength.

It's all right. Digital marketing isn't what you got into business to do.

The truth is you don't have enough time in the day, nor the inclination to stay on top of the latest emerging digital trends.

We could go on.

The problem is you've spent about half an hour reading over 5,000 words, and all we've done is either further enlightened you, or deeply depressed you about the uphill battle your brand marketing is facing today.

Honestly, we could go on to talk in depth about the latest Google algorithm updates, search engine optimization, inbound content marketing, and the fact that less than 15% of the followers of your free Facebook business page see your daily posts.

To continue would seriously leave you screaming, yelling and throwing your hands up in utter frustration at your plight. We know what you're up against on a daily basis.

Do you know the sad reality of all of this?

Most brick and mortar businesses cannot come anywhere near their marketing objectives due to limited budgets, lack of knowledge of how to coordinate the tools at their disposal, and the nature of the rapidly evolving marketing landscape. So where does that leave you?

You're Exactly Where You Need to Be!

You should have a real hunger to take back the control of your marketing.

You should be able to resist falling for every new and shiny marketing ploy that comes down the road.

You shouldn't be held emotionally hostage to the latest fads that you hear about in the news.

In short, what follows will give you a chance to open your eyes to the one-on-one marketing strategies that should be the cornerstone of your business. Get ready to learn from your mistakes. Many may have cost you thousands of dollars, untold hours of aggravation, and robbed your business of real growth over past years.

The struggle you face is real.

The future success of your business is on the line.

Let's seize this opportunity for change right now!

Chapter Three

A DISRUPTIVE, CLEAN-SHEET APPROACH TO MARKETING

"We cannot solve our problems with the same thinking we used when we created them."
—*Albert Einstein*

FIRST, WE SHOWED YOU THE PASSION GEN-
erated by the highly successful $12 billion dollar NFL sports league juggernaut.

We followed that up with shedding a white-hot spotlight on John Wanamaker's famous quote, "Half the money I spend on advertising is wasted, the trouble is I don't know which half," by actually showing you the hidden pitfalls and real barriers you're facing today with your marketing budget.

All of that information is great, but of little use, if you don't know what to do with it.

More importantly, how can you take what you've learned and make the actual changes that will give you the results your business has to have right now?

What's the answer?

Sometimes you have to start fresh with a clean-sheet approach to a problem, or as they say in the world of venture capitalists and Silicon Valley entrepreneurs, a disruptive approach.

Thanks to Clayton M. Christensen back in 1995 for defining a phenomenon of innovation he termed, "Disruptive Innovation."

Disruptive innovation is a process where a concept, product, or service takes root at the bottom of a market through early adopters. The innovation is so fundamentally better than what is currently being used by the market that it begins to move up the market relentlessly. It engulfs market share until it eventually displaces its established competitors.

Disruptive marketing is to approach the concept of marketing with a fresh, entirely clean-sheet approach.

As we discussed in Chapter Two, if you choose to follow the traditional marketing paths of others, don't be surprised when you end up ultimately with the same limitations and constraints they face now.

Don't want to buy into the disruptive approach to innovation? Don't think it has the power to change an industry?

Before you disregard it, you might want to consider a few of these relatively recent disruptions.

Five Quick Examples of Industry Disruption

1. Cellphones. Does anyone remember what a telephone booth looked like anymore?

2. iBooks, Kindle, Nook, and the book industry. What happened to Walden Bookstore?
3. Google Wallet, Paypal, Bitcoin, Apple Pay. Is cash soon to be a thing of the past?
4. iTunes for music. Do you buy CDs anymore? Can you even find them?
5. Netflix, Amazon Prime Video, Hulu, and countless others for movie consumption on-demand.

The question isn't whether disrupting your current marketing approach will work, the question is, "Are you truly ready for a change?" Are you tired of paying for lackluster results? Do you feel your marketing needs to be better at reaching your target audience?"

If you've read all of this and you don't think you should change your marketing, that's all right. We understand completely; you're busy and the natural thing to do is simply continue doing what you've done for years and hope for better results.

Ultimately, we have to warn you about that kind of thinking. Albert Einstein said it best, "The definition of insanity is doing the same thing over and over again and expecting a different result each time."

But we know you can do better!

In fact, you must do better because the future of your business hinges on being able to convey your brand story to your clients in a fragmented, entertainment-rich environment.

We've combined what makes the NFL such a perennial powerhouse of marketing, with a "clean-sheet disruptive" marketing style approach.

The entire program is designed from the ground up for a brick and mortar business. The result?

The Four Grainer "Actively Involved Marketing" (A.I.M.) Program

We termed it "Actively Involved Marketing" (A.I.M.) because, for once, control of your marketing program is in your hands. You have total control over the cost, profitability, and ultimate impact it makes with your clients.

We've boiled down the essence of marketing, stripped away all of the hype, hyperbole, and endless reams of esoteric marketing theories to reveal a program that works for every single brick and mortar location. The program will always work because of one essential truth in marketing, "People want to buy from people they know, like and trust."

The problem with advertising methods often used today is they seldom help you make the one-on-one connection you need.

In our search for the mythical "silver bullet" of marketing many have forgotten what we've always known in our heart and that is …

… The strongest business connections are made face-to-face with a client.

The A.I.M. program is designed from the ground up to drive people to your store so they can meet you.

They get a chance to hear firsthand from you about what your business is all about. Think for a moment about how profoundly powerful this is!

We spent the last chapter talking about the various media outlets like print, radio, television, social media, and the Internet "pushing" our brand message to clients. That's all well and good (except for the myriad pitfalls we outlined), but, what clever ad campaign can convey more emotion and passion about your business than you can while engaging with a client face to face?

Nothing in marketing trumps the one-on-one engagement with a potential client who is standing directly in front of you. Absolutely nothing does.

The bottom line goal for all your marketing efforts is to influence consumers enough to buy from you. What better opportunity is there then when the customer is standing right in front of you?

Of course, this begs the question, Don't you think it's about time we started talking about actually taking control of your marketing? It seems like all we've done to this point is complained about the problem without offering a solution.

And you know what Teddy Roosevelt says about that. "Complaining about a problem without proposing a solution is called whining."

That changes right now.

There'll be no whining here.

Let's take A.I.M. at your solution!

Chapter Four

WHAT EXACTLY IS ACTIVELY INVOLVED MARKETING?

*"That's been one of my mantras—Focus & Simplicity.
Simple can be harder than complex; you have to work
hard to get your thinking clean to make it simple "*
—Steve Jobs

SOMETHING SIMPLE THAT WORKS IS FAR better than something complicated and intellectually impressive that doesn't.

A.I.M. is a simple, everyday program that will work in your store to generate sales and enhance the positive image of your business in the community.

First, we're going to establish common ground by giving you an overview of "Actively Involved Marketing" (A.I.M.). Second, we'll introduce you to the features of this unique program and third, we'll end with answers to the top most asked questions.

Actively Involved Marketing Overview

The A.I.M. program is a complete marketing platform that partners with local charities to drive a full range of clients to your store. It's an incentive-based program energizing local charities to send supporters to your store.

Charities are always looking for donations and stores are always looking for new clients. When's the last time *you* called a charity and told them your store would like to make a donation? When's the last time you made someone's day by saying "yes" when solicited for a gift in person?

Well, it's time to start making as many donations as possible.

Wait, what?

How's giving going to get me clients? Easy, tie the size of the donation to the number of supporters visiting your store.

Most charities and local organizations have ways of reaching their fan base and encouraging them to visit your store to receive a larger donation. Locals wishing to support their favorite community-based charity are urged to visit your brick and mortar store and show their support by signing in a book.

Here's how you do it, in a nutshell: your store sets up a Community Outreach Program three ring binder with tabs for registered 501(c)3 charities. Local supporters sign in by providing their name, address, telephone number and email address on a page listing their preferred charity. You thank them for supporting local charities and let them know they've been added to your email list.

The more supporters sign up, the larger your donation, and the larger your customer base.

At the end of the defined sign up time, a donation is made to the charity based solely on the number of supporters the charity can rally to come into your store. The store's donation is always given in the form of gift certificates for goods, services, or merchandise at full retail value, never in cash.

But how does the A.I.M. program help your brick and mortar store?

Top Real-World Benefits to the A.I.M. Program.

First and foremost, this program:

- Drives people into your store.
- Brings in new clients who've never visited your store.
- Compels former customers to come back.
- Generates sales from supporters shopping in your store after they sign the book.
- Has costs, results, and profits that are 100% measurable.
- Is ideal for list building by getting the name, address, telephone #, and email address of everyone who visits your store.
- Provides content that engages and grows your various social media platforms organically.
- Costs less than $20 initially to set up and only pennies every year to maintain.
- Produces positive word of mouth advertising from the far-reaching public relations goodwill generated by supporting local charities.

- Creates a strong sense of pride among your organization's team members and greater overall teamwork because of it.
- Is the first marketing program you've ever used that gives you complete control over every facet of the operation.

We know what you're thinking right now. You're saying to yourself, "Hold on, this is too simple to work—and besides no one cares about local charities."

Before you stop reading, consider this one point: we wouldn't have spent so long producing this book if it didn't work. Our time would have been better spent doing one of a hundred things instead of writing a book about something that just sounds good in theory. Clearly, we aren't going to make a million dollars from book sales; there will be no lucrative cross-country speaking tour, and Tom Hanks won't be playing us in the movie adaptation.

We can say this program works because we've seen it work. Witnessed with our own eyes. Experienced the way it's changed the community's view of the store, energized the staff, and watched as the additional sales got rung up.

Change is good, and evolving the way we interact with the local charities can pay big dividends down the road. Saying "Yes" feels way better than saying "No."

Effective marketing, directed through local charitable organizations, lets you have the impact and reach larger companies pay millions to achieve.

So with that in mind, on to your questions.

Most Asked Questions About The A.I.M. Program

Question #1. I already support charities, and it hasn't done a thing for my business

That's an accurate statement, especially given the way most retailers traditionally give to a charitable organization. Your brick and mortar business is most likely approached on a weekly basis to give to one of the various local charities. Often, you succumb to the pressure and offer a nominal gift certificate which they raffle off, or donate a small item begrudgingly. Sometimes you get your logo on a flyer, T-shirt, or yearbook page and feel like you're supporting the community.

It's not that you hate to give. The problem is giving in the past has done almost nothing to drive business into your store. You just didn't know how to donate where both you and the charity benefited. Fortunately, the A.I.M. program shows you step by step how to turn this into a win-win situation.

Next up on the list would be this one.

Question #2. I never know how much to give

Good question, and one that everyone struggles with today. Not knowing appropriate donation amounts is why large businesses do their charitable giftings on a national basis. They take that burden off of their local stores and control the expense themselves.

When you're asking yourself, "How much should I give to each charity?" what you're doing is trying to answer the fundamental questions of fairness, as well as your Return On Investment (ROI).

You want your local community to perceive your business as equally giving to each charity. How do you make that determination? Is the 5k run for the local elementary school as important as the national breast cancer walk? Obviously, this depends on who you're talking to at the time.

The ROI question is valid because, at the end of the day, you're a business and you can't just give everything you have away without a reasonable return of some sort. But when considering ROI don't focus solely on the cost of the item you're donating, look at the level of exposure your gift will generate.

Fortunately, the A.I.M. program will determine how much to give the minute you set it up. In fact, we've devoted Chapter Nine, "How Much Do You Donate Per Person," to answering this question.

On to the next question on our top list.

Question #3. How much does the A.I.M. program cost to set up?

Fair question, especially in light of the hundreds of dollars your other marketing options usually cost to set up.

The initial cost is about $20.

In fact, here is a list of everything you need to get set up.

- A high quality 2" - 3" binder with a clear presentation type cover.

- 12 tab dividers, Avery three ring binder style.
- 50 pre-printed 8 ½ by 11 pages to distribute between the tab dividers.

After the first year, the good news is you can reuse the binder and tab dividers, so the expense drops the second year to just the cost of the paper sign up sheets.

We will go into detail of how to set up this binder and what goes on the pre-printed 8 ½ by 11-inch page in the "Physically Setting Up The A.I.M. Program," in Chapter Seven of this book.

Next question.

Question #4. How do I control the expenses and determine the ROI of this program?

Chapter Eight, "Setting The Record Straight About Marketing & ROI" is devoted to cost control and determining the ROI of this program. In the meantime, here's a very quick, 10,000-foot flyby.

You control costs primarily through the initial parameters you'll use to set up the program, and then adjustments you'll make throughout the year. These parameters become a way to limit both the number of charities applying and the amount they can raise for their event.

A quick list of parameters for controlling costs (which will be discussed in greater detail later) would include:

- The length of the form the charity has to fill out. Longer forms weed out weaker, less organized charities because they won't take the time to fill it out.

- Only allowing 501(c)3 charities to apply.
- Blackout dates for applying to the program.
- The number of days a charity has to drive their supporters to your store to sign the book.
- The amount per person you give to the charity.

You have total control over all the variables of the A.I.M. program, which—when you think about it—may mark the first time you've ever had a marketing program that gives you so much control over the number of new clients coming into your store and the expenses surrounding the program.

Now about that ROI part of the question.

Everyone asks about ROI, but the real issue should be, "What is the A.C.T. value of the program?"

Four Grainer developed the "Acquired Customer Traffic" (A.C.T.) formula to directly and accurately measure the effectiveness of any segment of your marketing program to drive traffic into your store.

In plain English, the expense of the Acquired Customer Traffic (A.C.T.) value represents the price you pay to acquire a full range of traffic through your front door.

As you remember, we define a full range of consumers as:

- Potential new buyers who've never been to your business.
- Former customers who haven't been to your store in over a year.

- Clients who've shopped at your location within the current year.

A.I.M. continually drives traffic to your store. It's up to you and your team to convert the A.C.T. into clients who buy things and retaining these customers is even more important. Marketers have seen that it costs five to ten times more to gain a new customer than to keep one who already trusts your business.

In its simplest form, A.C.T. can be worked out by this formula:

Divide the total costs associated with increasing foot traffic to your store by the total number of people who came into your store within a particular period.

Example, if you spent $1,000 on a magazine ad last month and ten people came into your store because of that ad, your A.C.T. cost is $100. ($1,000 divided by 10 = $100.)

The most important key metric to track when measuring the effectiveness of your marketing campaign is the cost to drive a full range of traffic into your store.

What separates our formula from others you've seen is, our sole focus is to drive a significant amount of people to your store. It's just that simple.

As always, it falls to your team to convert this full range of traffic into buying customers today, and long-term clients for life.

The A.C.T. number is a very handy tool to evaluate each of your ongoing marketing efforts. With it, you can quickly compare apples to apples in your marketing portfolio. You can determine which of your marketing efforts are making the grade by driving people into your store, and which ones are falling short. Chapter Eight provides more detail.

On to the next question on our list.

Question #5. Why do you only partner with 501(c)3 charities?

Your view of charitable giving has to change today. For years you've given thousands of dollars of your goods and services away with little, if any, tangible return on your investment. From now on you have to view your donation as forming a partnership between your business and the charitable organization. A partnership where both parties win.

The best way for you to win?

Partner with the most committed, best-organized charities in your area, and those are 501(c)3 charities. Charities with this designation have already been vetted as a legitimate charitable organization by the state. More importantly, they're audited and continually scrutinized by the state's IRS for compliance.

By declaring that for IRS purposes, your business only donates to 501(c)3 charities, the burden's been lifted from you to give to every bake sale and lemonade stand in the area.

On to probably the most important question of all.

Question #6. Honestly, does the A.I.M. program work?

Without hesitation, the answer is a resounding, emphatic "YES!"

It works on the financial end of the equation because it is the least expensive means to acquire new clients. From strictly the advertising point of view, nothing helps your business make a personal connection to new customers faster than being face-to-face in your store.

Not only does A.I.M. drive hundreds of people into your business every year, more importantly, it also brings your communities most affluent and influential clients.

Print, radio, TV, Internet, social media, direct mail—nothing, and we do mean nothing, puts the power of connecting with your clients in your hands like A.I.M.

It gives you the opportunity to represent your "brand" with everyone the charity has driven to your store.

So What's Next?

So we've given you the mission statement for A.I.M. and answered the top questions most small businesses have about the basics of the program. All of this is all well and good, but until you've experienced the program in action, you can't fully appreciate it.

If you can't visualize how A.I.M. will work in your store, then you probably aren't going to finish this book and probably won't set it up. So what we're going to do is take a break and let the clients and the staff of the store tell you about the program in their words.

It's vital that you get a genuine feel for the program and experience the many layers that it has to support your business.

Nothing fancy here, we're just going to lay it out in a straight narrative form, undiluted, and unaltered.

After you hear about what the program means to the people who use it, we'll pick back up and answer the next burning question which is, "Are your clients truly passionate about charities?"

See you on the other side.

Chapter Five

A FLY ON THE WALL—WHAT CLIENTS & STAFF SAY ABOUT THE PROGRAM

"I succeeded by saying what everyone else was thinking"
—Comedian Joan Rivers.

I T'S EASY TO GET WRAPPED UP IN STATS AND theories, in fact, most business and marketing books get bogged down doing it all the time. The problem is you read the various best-selling books and get excited about putting their theories into action at your location. You spend time figuring out how to adapt it to your store, and then just before you launch it, this nagging voice of doubt starts to whisper questions in your head.

"Will my clients see the advantage?"

"Will it financially grow my business at the end of the day?"

"The theory is intuitive in the book, but will it work here, with *our* clients?"

Have to say, we had those same voices whispering to us before we started.

Wouldn't it be nice if, for once, you could be a fly on the wall in some other store that was using the program today? In this particular case, to hear what the people said after they signed the community outreach book. That's what this chapter is going to do.

Before we show you how to set up the A.I.M. program, we're going to share why you should set it up in the first place. We're going to give you real world conversations in a simple, straightforward dialog manner. Nothing fancy, just the essence of the genuine conversation, in no particular order. Just one snippet of conversation at a time. In the end, you can be the judge if you want your clients responding the same way in your brick and mortar store.

First up will be the responses we've overheard from the clients.

Client's Response

CLIENT: It's great that you support so many local charities. You know, since I'm here, I've got an anniversary coming up and...

CLIENT (after signing the book): You know I haven't been in here in years. Oh, I didn't know you sold ABC product, when did you start selling it...?

CLIENT: We can't thank you enough for your support of our charity. It's hard to find businesses anymore that care about the community. I'll be back because I want to support businesses that support the community...

CLIENT: I didn't know your business was even here. I had to look it up on Google to find it so I could come in to sign the book...

CLIENT: You know, I've always heard your merchandise was so expensive when compared to your competition. Since I'm here, I can see that's not true...

CLIENT: Thanks for giving a donation to the charity. I've lived in the area for six years but have never stopped in. . .

CLIENT: Great of you to support our charity. Do you guys fix or carry...?

CLIENT: Can't tell you how much it means to me that you support the ABC charity. (Tears start to well up in her eyes.) You know my daughter died of...

CLIENT: How long have you been supporting local charities? You know, I haven't been back to this store since you all stopped carrying... (The good news is that we were able to show the client a new line we just got in that was similar.)

CLIENT, referring to the ease of signing the book to support her charity: Well that was easy! While I'm here, I might as well look around...

CLIENT: So glad I made it in today to sign the book. The charity has been sending out email blasts every few days telling us to make time to get in here to sign...

CLIENT (a chairperson for one of the local charities): I knew I had to get in here to sign the book because I've been emailing and texting everyone else all week to stop by your store.

CLIENT: Signing this book was as easy as they said it was. By the way, have you seen all of the postings on Facebook our charity has done to get people to come into your store to sign the book...?

CLIENT (a superintendent of a local faith-based church and school): We've sent out an email blast every week this month to everyone associated with the school and church. In fact, for the past three Sunday services, the pastor has gotten up and told everyone they have to come to your store and sign the book before our 30-day window is up.

CLIENT (a supporter of a local charity asked after she signed the book): How close are we to the next donation level? Wow, we're that close? Do you mind if I just sort of stand over here and send out a few texts to get people to come in to sign? (For the record, she got five more people to come into the store that day.)

CLIENT: You probably don't remember me, but I signed the book last year for ABC charity. I told my husband last year he had to buy my Christmas gift from you, and he did!

CLIENT: Your store is so generous to support our charity. I tell all my friends about your store now.

CLIENT: You know, I won a $200 gift certificate last year from your store at the charity auction. It helped towards my anniversary gift!

CLIENT: I was telling all of my friends on Facebook how lucky we are to have a local business that supports our charity...

CLIENT: I don't make it over to this side of town very much, but I just had to come over to sign the book. I didn't know your store was even here... (For the record, she lived less than 5 miles away.)

Those 20 sincere responses from clients are representative of the hundreds that we could have listed. They give you a sense of the power of the program to touch the hearts of the supporters in a positive, passionate way. The takeaway from these comments is that they were sincere and unsolicited.

Those same sentiments could have been voiced in your brick and mortar store just as easily. Whatever the retail product you sell or line of services you provide, the genuineness of those emotions would be the same.

Now let's flip the coin and listen in to the responses from the staff.

Staff's Response

STAFF: It makes me feel good to be working for a business that is giving back to the community.

STAFF: Thanks for supporting ABC charity! I see it's been a few years since you've been in the store, let me show what we just got in.

STAFF: Yes, I know, it's great that we're able to give back to the community that's supported us for all of these years.

STAFF: Welcome back! Thanks for signing the book for ABC charity. How did your husband like the gift you got him last week?

STAFF: Thanks for supporting the charity, did you say you've never been in before? Oh my gosh, let me show you around!

STAFF: Oh, of course, I'll take a photo with your phone of you signing the book to show your friends.

STAFF: I love it when people come in to sign the book. They always say how thankful they are that the store supports their charity.

STAFF: I can't believe how much business we get from people signing the book.

STAFF: You know, I see some of the people who signed the book a couple of weeks ago coming back to the store to buy something.

STAFF: Have you read some of the great comments the charities are leaving on their Facebook pages about our store?

Powerful phrases and sentiments indeed from the staff.

It would be difficult to imagine a store not wanting to hear those comments from their team members and the people coming into their store.

We could have filled several chapters on the warm, heartfelt responses from the people who came to sign the book. The personal stories they shared, the genuine gratitude they conveyed, convinced us immediately that we had something with the A.I.M. program that was unique.

You'll never experience this level of personal interaction from traditional marketing, nor from social media.

In an era of, "What's in it for me?" there is something very cathartic in giving back to those in your local community who are in need. The reciprocity in turn of the town giving back to the store was something we didn't know would happen when we started the program.

Perhaps we were jaded by life, perhaps made cynical by the selfishness of the people we read about daily in the media. But, we were wrong, and in so many ways, disappointed in ourselves for not anticipating the caring inner nature of the people in the area.

It's hard to point out who benefits more from the A.I.M. program. Is it the volunteers who feel good about doing something that benefits their charity?

Could it be the staff who have this greater sense of pride about their store, and deeper connection with clients?

Perhaps it's the management team that gets the emotional boost from all the positive energy flowing from the hundreds of people thanking them for supporting the local community?

Or, the business itself that receives a needed boost of traffic through the front door, and the subsequent sales benefit from that traffic?

Perhaps, in this instance, everyone walks away as a winner.

***

While we're talking about being a fly on the wall, this would be a good time to pass along a quick story of one customer who came in to sign for his favorite charity.

The staff noticed that he wrote "4" in the "Years" section and asked him why it had been four years since his last visit to the store.

This client's answer epitomizes the real value of the A.I.M. program to drive a full range of customers to your store.

His response is one that should cause every store owner or manager to take a moment and contemplate.

Here's his story.

While this man was writing down the required information, we asked him if he had ever visited the store before. His reply was that he used to be a long-time client of the business, but he had stopped shopping here because of an incident.

When he was asked about the incident, he said that four years ago he had intended to purchase a gift card from the store to give to his wife on their anniversary. Their anniversary was on a Sunday, and while he had every good intention of coming in on Friday, he had gotten tied up with work and just forgotten about it until early Sunday morning.

Apparently, they were having a big anniversary party at their house with their children and grandchildren that day.

Panicked, he jumps into his car and drives over to the store at 10:00 am on a Sunday to pick up a gift certificate.

The problem for him was that the store opened at noon on Sunday. In his mind, the store wasn't open when he desperately needed it to be open, and that was the issue.

He had to go home and listen to his wife tell their grown children and their spouses that afternoon how he was too busy with work to find the time to pick up her anniversary gift.

Was it the store's fault?

Clearly not, but after he picked up the gift card from the store the following week, he never came back to shop there. That's how little it takes to lose a customer—it can be a minor inconvenience, something completely justifiable from your perspective, but something unforgivable from the client's point of view.

It wasn't until he came to sign the A.I.M. book that we finally had a chance to hear the story and apologize for not being open when he needed us.

The bottom line is that he would never have come back to the store if we hadn't had this opportunity to reconnect over our A.I.M. program.

He needed a reason to return that was stronger than any cleverly worded glossy magazine advertisement could provide.

There wasn't a hook, a gimmick or discount that would have moved him, except for his desire to support this worthwhile community charity.

The store spent thousands and thousands of dollars in advertising during the four years since he had been in the store, and it never moved him.

All too often we expect our professionally prepared advertising to speak to the hearts of our clients for us. We forget the cardinal rule of selling which is: "People buy from people they know, like, and trust."

Fortunately, the store was able to gain back the client because the connection was re-established, and sales are now coming in because of it. This speaks to the essence of what the A.I.M. program is all about.

The program is unique because it gives you the precious face to face opportunities with current, prior, and potentially new clients that are *everything* to a small business.

No other means of advertising can do this with such profound impact as this program. We've witnessed the bonds formed between client and business first hand.

What should keep you awake at night after reading about this one client is the thought of how many clients like him are out there for your business?

What if you had a second chance?

What if they came back into your store and you had another opportunity to talk to them? To make wrongs right again, or at the least stop your team from making the same mistake again?

What would that mean to you and your business?

To borrow a line from the classic MasterCard commercial: Priceless.

We hope this chapter has given you greater insight into the emotions the A.I.M. program evokes in clients and the staff.

There is still one burning question to be answered before we jump into how to setup the program: "Are clients truly passionate about charities?"

We can all agree that the NFL has passionate fans across the U.S. but can local charities elicit that same level of excitement?

The answer will astound you.

Chapter Six

THE NFL VS. CHARITIES—
NOT EVEN CLOSE

"No one has ever become poor from giving."
—*Anne Frank*

OUTSIDE OF THE WORLD OF SPORTS, VERY little stirs people like rallying together to support a local charity. Charitable functions draw people from all walks of life, and all socioeconomic backgrounds. These people donate their precious time and give their financial assistance in support of a common cause.

Or so you would think, but is that true in today's world, the world where teenagers who are sitting in the same room send an electronic message to each other instead of having a face to face conversation?

The question we're asking is simply, "Do Americans still support charities?"

They do and in a big way.

Americans gave an estimated $358.38 billion to charity in 2014, surpassing the peak last seen before the 2008 Great Recession, according to the 60th-anniversary edition of Giving USA. The $358.38 billion represents the largest amount donated to charities in the 60 years Giving USA has been publishing their annual report.

Take a moment to consider the $358.38 billion revenue taken in for charitable organizations versus the $12 billion revenue of the NFL.

It's true that Americans assign importance with their wallets, and in this case, charities are 29 times more important than the NFL. The overall size of our charitable contributions is a testament to the importance Americans place on helping others who are less fortunate.

Both the NFL and local charities have fans who are genuinely invested emotionally in the outcome.

While they probably won't be wearing licensed NFL gear, many will be wearing pink ribbon lapel pins or event T-shirts to show their solidarity.

In fact, the NFL has borrowed heavily from the playbook (if you will) of religious and charitable organizations to ignite the intense passion of their fan base.

The high-powered marketing brain trust of the NFL has purposely developed engagement that is designed to connect to their fans; however, even the mighty NFL pales in comparison to local charities in the way they pluck our emotional heartstrings.

Do you doubt the power of charitable organizations to move people to action?

The Earth Moving Power of Charities

There are hundreds of examples we could draw on to demonstrate the power of people coming together to support a common cause. From the neighborhood child who needs to raise money for life-saving surgery to thousands of people across the country who actively support Breast Cancer Awareness every year. Our generosity and support are not limited to humans: it extends to animals as well.

The Influence of the ASPCA

Between 37% to 47% of all households own a dog in America, according to the American Society for the Prevention of Cruelty to Animals (ASPCA). How committed are those active members to raising awareness to the overt cruelty and appalling plight of some animals in this country? The ASPCA routinely receives tens of millions of dollars in donations for its important work in protecting animals.

Have you seen the Sarah McLachlan ASPCA "Angel" commercials that aired in the late 90's? Even Sarah herself says that she has to turn the channel because they touch such an emotional spot with her. Though apparently, they stirred the emotions of more people than just Sarah. She revealed that those ads alone had raised over $30 million for the ASPCA.

Our charitable love is certainly not limited to animals, though.

Remember the Jerry Lewis Labor Day Telethon?

The history of the Muscular Dystrophy Association telethon goes all the way back to the 1950s when Jerry Lewis would host a Thanksgiving Party for MDA to aid the organization's New York City area operations financially.

The Labor Day telethon that many of us remember ran from 1966 through 2009 and raised $2.45 billion dollars for the charity.

The telethon, which started on a Sunday evening preceding Labor Day, was broadcast for up to 21 hours through late Monday afternoon on the national holiday itself.

Millions tuned in every year to share an emotional experience that was larger than themselves and to give their support to a worthy cause.

The MDA appropriately called its network of participating stations the "Love Network."

For 28 years the MDA telethon broadcasted from Las Vegas, Nevada, and they evoked the kind of heartfelt compassion that remained long after the television is turned off.

The kind of sentiment that convicts you in your heart to generously give your time and volunteer to raise money and awareness for this worthy cause.

We are a nation of compassionate people. Americans have always been charitable and kind to those less fortunate.

Almost every day total strangers fearlessly walk into our brick and mortar locations asking for donations to support their favorite charities.

They come into our stores because they want us to join them in the struggle to overcome a specific dilemma facing our community.

They present to us a rare opportunity to transcend the transactional.

To be more than a brick and mortar warehouse for goods and services.

To be elevated from a servant status to that of an equal in this daunting local struggle, and in doing so, change the perception of your business in their eyes.

Can you put a quantitative price on what that change in attitude means to the short and long-term success of your business?

***

So here we are.

We've learned about the almost insurmountable marketing challenges facing independent businesses today.

We know from experience that the most effective marketing takes place face-to-face in our stores.

We've been a fly on the wall as we overheard from actual clients and team members about how the store's Community Outreach Program moved them in so many positive ways.

Lastly, we've discussed how people take action, both on a national and local level in support of a charitable organization that touches their heart.

Now we just need to set up the A.I.M. program physically.

Don't stress out. It won't take long, because as always, we keep it simple.

Besides. Don't let the fear of the unknown keep you from changing what you know doesn't work.

We both know it's time for a change.

Chapter Seven

PHYSICALLY SETTING UP THE A.I.M. PROGRAM

*"The difference between something good and
something great is attention to detail."*
—Charles R. Swindoll

W E'RE FINALLY HERE.
The place where the rubber meets the road in your drive to retake control of your marketing.

You've gotten all the facts, stats, and background information you need. Now it's time to build it, because, in this instance, if you build it, they will come.

Let's start with the physical setup of the program.

As we mentioned in Chapter Four, the cost to set up the program is a maximum of $20 initially.

Since you can reuse the binder and tab dividers every year, the expense drops in subsequent years to just the cost of the paper signup sheets.

Always keep in mind the outcome doesn't hinge on a hand-stitched Corinthian leather bound binder with your business's name hand embossed with gold leaf on the cover. It hinges on your ability to make a connection with the full range of people this program drives to your store's doorstep.

Focus on what is essential to the success of this program, the details that matter.

Everything You Need to Get Set Up

Item Number One: Nice quality binder

We bought one from the local Staples which was a heavy-duty 3-inch slant-D 3-ring view binder in black.

The item number is 82669 / model: 24690-US, priced at $11.49.

It is important to get a heavy duty binder because you are going to be using it several times a day.

We got one with a clear page insert option for the front and back for a graphical page about the program that we designed. The clear back page portion is there for a quick recap page of the program and the various contribution levels.

> ****SIGNIFICANT**** Part of your presentation to the charity supporters who come into your store is in letting them know how important each person increases the amount of the donation to the charity and how close they are to attaining the next donation level. This information helps to keep the charity volunteers excited about the program.
>
> In fact on several occasions, after they finished signing the book, we've seen them stop, pull out their phone and text others to come in saying, "We're so close to the next level!"
>
> This simple point indeed drives excitement.

Item Number Two: One set of Avery three ring binder style, 12 tab dividers

This tab divider doesn't have to be an Avery product, just as long as it's a three ring binder, 12 tab divider style.

We used Avery Ready Index Numbered Tab Dividers, 12-Tab—Assorted Colors—Labeled 1-12—3-Hole Punched—Paper—1 Set/ Pack.

Customizable table of contents. Product Number: AVE 11843 which we found online for $2.87.

Some have asked us, "Why do you use numbered tabs, and why multi-colored ones?"

Yes, we could have gone with a product that would have allowed us to print the name of the charity on it. While it would have been a nice touch, it isn't needed, and it wouldn't have been reusable.

Why numbered tabs? When you get this program up and running, you will be having multiple charities signing the book at the same time.

The numbered tabs also send a powerful nonverbal message that your company is supporting numerous charities in your local community.

Why multi-colored tabs? Granted it does add a splash of color, but more importantly, it is a mnemonic memory device that aids information retention in the human memory. The volunteer often remembers the color and the number of the tab they signed under and can relay it back to others who are coming in later to sign the book.

Item Number Three: The actual signup page for the charity

This page will be in the three ring binder, under the colored, numbered tab for their organization.

The key here is simplicity and legibility.

At this junction, we are making the assumption that you have access to a word processor program on your computer.

If not, an old-fashioned typewriter that you have sitting around collecting dust somewhere will work equally well.

At this point, we are going to create the master signup page.

After that, we will make copies of this master in the future as we need them.

Remember that you will have volunteers of all ages coming into your store to sign the book, so a readable font size of 12 or 13 points is an important consideration as is the clarity of the font style.

We recommend a standard, highly legible TrueType font such as Times Roman, Helvetica, Courier, or Arial.

What a Signup Page Would Look Like

** If you would like to save time, we have a downloadable PDF file already developed for you. It's free at https://goo.gl/q8oVOa

Title at the top would be "[Your Store's Name] Community Outreach Program."

While we're here, let's talk about the phrase "Community Outreach Program."

The total A.I.M. program has several components, one of which we are focusing on here is called, Community Outreach Program.

Four Grainer developed the A.I.M. program to be an overarching umbrella for a series of programs specifically designed to give you back complete control over your marketing.

The Community Outreach Program is what you would call this specific program on your website when mentioning it in email marketing, on your social media platforms, with staff, etc.

2nd line would be "Charity Name" followed by an area to handwrite the charity's name, followed by "Contact Person" followed by a space to handwrite the contact's name.

3rd line would be, "Start Date" followed by an area to handwrite the start date that volunteers and supporters can come in to sign the book, followed by "Ending Date" and the needed space to write the ending date.

4th line would be the start of the general rules.

We used bold print here on all of the general requirements and aligned them into two columns.

The First Rule Is "Must Be at Least 18 Years Old to Sign Up"

You must have a disclaimer on each page that clearly says that you must be over 18 years of age or older to sign this book.

The very last thing your business needs is to have the name, address, phone number and email address of minors added to your marketing efforts.

Seriously, a word to the wise should be sufficient here.

Next Rule: "The Complete Form Must Be Filled Out to Qualify"

Some people don't want to give out their email address or telephone number, which is understandable in today's world, but here's the rub.

The information in this block is how you are going to grow your email list, direct mail programs, and future general marketing efforts.

In essence, this is an important part of how your business gets paid for your charitable donations, so hold fast to this rule.

You can't berate someone for not putting down all of the information.

You should, however, tell them the information is for in-house marketing purposes only and that your company will not sell or provide that information to others.

Another point to bring up is that at the completion of the signup period, the charity receives a copy of the signup pages. You do this to provide transparency but also so that the charity knows who to thank for coming in to sign the book.

It's been our experience that the rare person who questions providing the required information will do so once you explain how important you regard the privacy aspect of their information and that the charity gets a copy of the signup pages.

The truth of the matter, however, is that it isn't your privacy policy that convinces them to fill in all of the blanks. It's because they want full credit for supporting the charity that ultimately sways them.

What do you do with that one rare person who still won't fill in all of the blocks?

Count him of course, and while it would be beneficial to your business to have all of the information, it just isn't worth looking cheap or overly-legalistic. Also keep in mind that a lot of the program's focus is just getting potential customers actually to come through your doors in the first place, and in that regard you've already succeeded.

In the two years of running the program, we didn't have one person come into the store that didn't sign the book.

Next Rule: "Can Only Sign for One Charity Per Year"

A slight percentage of the community actively support more than one charity.

What you're trying to avoid is someone coming in to sign for the one charity and at the same time taking the opportunity to sign for some other charities as well.

This potential problem is easy to avoid if you are talking to them while they are signing.

The Last General Rule: "You Will Be Added To Our Mailing List"

The rest of the page is for the signup blocks.

By adjusting the font size between 12 or 13, and the page layout, you should be able to put five sign up blocks on each page.

A typical sign up block would be:

Print Name:
Address:
Email Address:
Telephone #:
Yrs:

So you simply take the above example and redo it several times down the page.

Make a real effort to get five fields per page because it saves you so much time in counting the number of people who signed up. You can just count the pages, rather than each block.

> ****SIGNIFICANT**** When you set up the first sign up page for a new charity, fill in the top portion and then make copies of that page. This tip saves you the time needed to complete the top section of every subsequent page for that charity.

The last part of the sign-up book has to do with the clear plastic inserts on the front and back of the heavy duty binder. We recommend that on the front cover insert you place a copy of the write-up about the Community Outreach Program that you've put on your website.

On the back of the binder in the clear plastic insert, we recommend putting in a quick reference sheet which shows the various levels of participation and the payout for those levels.

Here again, make the general font large enough to be easily read with no fine print.

As a means of example, a typical generic signup page would look like this, of course depending on the device you're using to read this ebook, the actual spacing could look off.

We know the form doesn't look perfect on every book format or e-reader, but we still included it as a way to give you a general overview of the page layout:

(Your Business Name) Community Outreach Program.

Charity Name:
Contact Person
Start Date:
Ending Date:

*Must Be Over 18 Years Old To Sign Up.
*Block Must Be Filled Out To Qualify.
*Only Sign Up For One Charity Per Year.
*You Will Be Added To Our Mailing List.

Print Name:
Address:
Email Address:
Telephone #:
Yrs:

SIGNIFICANT Yrs: ___ Is a vital bit of information to acquire.

What we are asking is, "How long has it been since you've been in the store?"

If they've never been to your store, then they would put "0."

For those who have been to the store within the past 12 months, they would put "1" regardless of the actual number of months.

In the instance where they haven't been back to the store for some time, then they would put down the number of years since their last visit.

On average it takes most store owners 20 to 30 minutes to set up this generic page, or less.

Now that you have the in-store signup form completed for your binder, next would be the one for the charitable organizations themselves.

They would fill out this form in its entity to sign up their 501(c)3 charity for your Community Outreach Program.

After two years of actually running the Community Outreach Program in a brick and mortar store, we can tell you without hesitation that a properly setup 501(c)3 Charitable Partner signup form is vital to a smooth running program.

At first glance, it may look daunting to fill out, but rest assured that every single item is there to minimize confusion between you and the charity while maximizing the ROI of your charitable donation.

Besides you aren't the one filling it out, and neither are those charities who aren't committed to growing their organization and in turn, growing your business.

In our experience, there is a direct correlation between the length of the form and the number of people the organization can drive into your store.

A longer form to fill out tends to weed out those charities who aren't well organized or motivated to send significant numbers of their supporters to your front door.

You will save yourself considerable time and have significantly greater success per charity if you use the form we've provided.

What follows is the actual "Charitable Partner" signup form we used.

We have a paper and an electronic version of this page. The paper copy is used to hand out to the volunteers while they are in our store. The other is an electronic version that we put on the business's website under the "Contact Us" tab.

Either way, the information required is the same.

In fact, if you see a "*" symbol after a request such as "Name of Organization:*" that means on the electronic version you had to fill in that block, or the form couldn't be submitted.

Obviously, once again, the layout of the form is much smaller space-wise so that it would work in this format. Your version would have the same verbiage, but more space to fill in the blanks.

So let's take a look at the form.

Charitable Partner Signup Form

* If you would like to save time, we have a download-able PDF file already developed for you. It's free at: https://goo.gl/q8oVOa

(Your Business Name) Community Outreach Program

Please fill out the form below so we can start the evaluation process for your 501(c)3 charity.

Only those charitable organizations that have submitted the Charity Partner form will be eligible for approval.

We make every effort to process the form within three of our business days.

Thank you for helping to make (Your Community Name Here) and the surrounding area a better place to live for all of us!

Today's Date:
ORGANIZATION INFORMATION
Name of Organization*:
Address of Organization*:
Street Address*:
Website for the Organization*:
Overall Description / Goals of the Organization
Please provide your 501(c)3 Tax ID number*:
When do you want to start your 30 day sign up period?*
When do you want to pick up the gift certificate?*
Who is going to pick up the gift certificate?—THIS INDIVIDUAL WILL BE THE ONLY PERSON WHO CAN COLLECT THE GIFT CERTIFICATE.

Name*

CONTACT INFORMATION—TWO ARE
REQUIRED
Are you the primary contact?
What is the best way to communicate with you?*
Name*
Email*
Phone*
Secondary Contact—Name*
Secondary Contact—Email*
Secondary Contact—Phone*

EVENT INFORMATION
Contribution / Donation deadline date*
Please give us an overview of the fundraiser*
Official title of the event*
Date of the event*
Start time of the event
Ending time of the event*
Address of the event*

Is there a separate website/landing page devoted to this
event? If so, please list.

Is there a separate contact email setup for the event?

What is the expected attendance at the event?

Has the organization received a donation from (Your
Business Name) in the past?

If so, what was the gift/amount?

How will the organization support the event? (i.e. Organization Website, Special Website / Landing Page, Facebook, Twitter, Special Email Campaign, etc.)

Please outline the strategy the organization will use to promote the event:

Please list the different levels of involvement you are making available to us.

Is there anything else you would like to share concerning this event?

Which of our social media outlets would you like us to use to support your event?

If you would like for us to support your event through our social media outlets, do we have permission to use your logo/event description to promote this event? Please outline limitations if any.

If you would like us to promote your event throughout social media outlets, how are you going to encourage your organization to support our social media through Facebook "Likes," followers to our Twitter account?

How will our donation / informational materials be displayed at the event?

When will we be notified of the winner(s) of our contribution?*

Please provide the name and email address of the winner(s) after the event so that we can congratulate them.

Who is going to pick up the contribution/donation?*

Date & time you are going to pick-up the contribution/ donation.*

AGREEMENT

By submitting this donation request form, I fully agree that any donation received is not to be used for resale and that all contributions/donations received from (Your Business Name Here) are for use by the organization noted above. I also state that I have the authority from the above-listed organization to enter into this agreement. My Name/address/phone and email address is listed as primary contact on this form.*

Agreement Signature / Date:

END—Today's Date[1]

***

Yes, we would have to agree with what you're thinking right now.

The Charity Partner signup form has some length to it.

The truth is you need every single line if you're going to get the most out of your time, financial investment, as well as minimize possible confusion.

As a side note, not one charity ever complained in two years about having to fill out the form, or the length of it.

---

1   Whenever you update the form change the date, so you know you've got the latest version.

As an Additional Bonus

We've added the following cover sheet that we used for the A.I.M. program.

The cover sheet outlines the basic program goals, the various levels, donation amounts, and frequently asked questions.

We used an electronic version for the website, while also having a print version in the store as a handout.

Obviously, there are some tremendous advantages to having both an electronic and a print version of the cover sheet and the actual Charitable Partner signup form available.

We've found that after the program has been running for a few months and the word spreads throughout your community, the electronic version was the preferred method for charities to apply for the program.

The electronic version was also handier for saving information for future reference, and for establishing an electronic paper trail.

We understand that putting the electronic signup form on your website will require getting with your website developer, but in our experience, the effort more than paid for itself.

If you opt for only a print version, please feel free to copy the actual form we used below.

Cover Sheet for The Community Outreach Program

Community Outreach Program

Thank you for considering (your store's name) as a potential charitable partner!

Last year we were fortunate to be able to sponsor many different charities in [your town] and surrounding areas.

This year we would like to be more generous in our support for even more local charities!

These challenging economic times make it difficult for charitable organizations to provide the services that our community relies upon throughout the year.

That is why we are giving approved 501(c)3 charities, regardless of size, the opportunity to receive a substantial donation from our business.

Your Charitable Organization is Important To Our Community!

We know you, and those in your charitable organization are passionate about helping others.

We would like the opportunity to meet them and personally thank them for donating their time and energy.

That is why we created the "Community Outreach Program."

How does the program work?

We believe in keeping it simple.

Step One: Fill out the Charitable Partner form, then contact our store manager at [store telephone #] to ensure everything is ready to go.

Step Two: Get the word out! Let everyone in your organization know they can make a direct impact on the amount of your donation simply by coming into [store name] and signing under your charity's tab in our Community Outreach Program book.

Your supporters simply have to be at least 18 years old, with a valid photo ID. They must sign under your charity's tab in our Community Outreach Program book with their name, address, email address, and telephone number.

All four pieces of information must be provided by the supporter to count in the charity's total.

Those who sign the book are added to our internal mailing list. The personal information they have provided is kept in strict confidence and is never shared with those outside of our organization.

The signup pages under your charity's tab allow us to keep track of your progress.

We will also provide your charitable organization with a copy of the physical record at the end of the signup period so you can thank your supporters.

Step Three: Call our store at [store telephone number] and speak to our store manager at least two business days before you want your gift certificate.

The Amount We Donate Is Completely Up To You And Your Members!

Here Are The First Five Levels:

Bronze Level—Receive a $100 gift certificate by having five people sign under your charity's tab in our store.

Silver Level—Receive a $250 gift certificate by having 6 to 10 people sign under your tab.

Gold Level—Receive a $500 gift certificate by having 11 to 15 people sign under your tab.

Platinum Level—Receive a $750 gift certificate by having 16 to 20 people sign under your tab.

Diamond Level—Receive a $1,000 gift certificate by having 21 to 25 people sign under your tab.

*** The good news is that we continue to increase your donation for every supporter you have over the Diamond Level!

Frequently Asked Questions (F.A.Q.)

What are the dates the Community Outreach Program is open? The program is set up on a calendar basis starting January 15th and running through October 31st.

How many days do we have to get to have our supporters in to sign under our charity's tab? Each charity can have a maximum 30-day window to get as many supporters as possible to come in and sign under your charity's tab.

If you don't need or don't have 30 days before your event, the shortest window is five of our business days.

Can we apply to be a Charitable Partner every year? Absolutely! All you have to do is re-submit your application between January 15th and October 20th.

Does the program reset each year? Yes. Your charity can apply once every year, and your supporters can sign up once every year.

When can we pick up our gift certificate for this year? Anytime between January 25th and December 31st during regular business hours.

We do require you to call the store at (store's telephone #) and speak to the store manager at least two of our work days before you come in to pick up your gift certificate so we can have it ready for you.

Can our members sign under more than one charity's tab? No. Only one signup per person per year. In the event of a discrepancy, or attempt to sign up for more than one program, we will delete that individual from every list that year.

Could someone sign under our charity's tab online, by telephone, fax, email, or by phone text? No. Only those who physically come into (your store name here).

What if we can't pick up our gift certificate before December 31st? Please contact our store manager at (store telephone #) before Dec 31st.

Can someone else pick up our gift certificate? No. Only the person/persons designated on the entry form can receive that charity's gift certificate.

Spouses, children of, relatives of, significant others of, or friends of the predesignated person/persons cannot pick up the gift certificate.

Only the person/persons predesignated with proper photo ID can receive the gift certificate.

Can we receive our gift certificate and put it in a blind auction/raffle it off / give it away? Yes, once you have physically picked up your gift certificate.

Can I substitute the gift certificate for cash? No, you cannot redeem it for money. The gift certificate is for merchandise, and services at (your store's name) only.

Can any charity sign up for the "Community Outreach Program"? Yes, any 501(c)3 charities can submit their Charitable Partner form. We will make every effort to determine if you've been approved within three of our business days.

Could this program be subject to change? Yes. This program can be altered, amended, or terminated by (your store's name) at any time without notice.

END—Today's Date

About the Three Forms

You're probably saying, "Okay, but my business is different than your test store, and those donation amounts wouldn't work for my business," and you would be right.

The real beauty of this program lies in its adaptability.

View the in-store signup sheet, the charitable partner signup sheet and this cover letter as a "best practices" template for your individual A.I.M. program.

Yes, these three forms were developed over two years of real world testing, but feel free to adapt them to the needs of your particular business.

While the cover sheet is set up for a store with a 50% margin, it can easily be adapted to work with any brick and mortar store simply by changing the dates, levels and the donation amounts as needed to suit your business's margin levels and marketing budget.

Of the three forms, the cover sheet is the only one most stores will need to adjust.

***

We've covered a lot of important ground in this chapter.

Thanks for hanging in there.

We're not making excuses, but it can be difficult even for a Pulitzer-winning author to describe how to put together a signup form and not cause a few yawns.

Think how hard it was for us!

At the end of the day, we know how important it is to take the time to show you how to physically setup the program.

But for the record, even we took a short nap halfway through.

The good news?

We're rolling down the home stretch now!

You should have the "Community Outreach Program" binder physically put together now with the individual charity tabs and sign-up sheets in place.

The program's cover page and the Charitable Partner sign-up form are now ready.

Though to be honest, you are probably a little uneasy about how the ROI is going to work out, and how to set the donation levels.

Next chapter let's hit the ROI question head on and while we're at it, sets the record straight about what marketing is, and what it isn't.

We said back in Chapter Two that "Knowledge is Power," well prepare yourself to get another power boost!

Chapter Eight

SETTING THE RECORD STRAIGHT ABOUT MARKETING & ROI

"Good marketing makes the company look smart.
Great marketing makes the customer feel smart."
—*Joe Chernov*

As we delve into the ROI aspects of the "Actively Involved Marketing" (A.I.M.) program, we have to take a moment and establish a common ground with regards to what the term "Marketing" means, and how we're going to measure the success of the program.

Now is a perfect time to set the record straight about what marketing is and more importantly, what it isn't.

This is the straightforward definition we use:

"Marketing is about attracting profitable customers to your business and retaining them."

The most important thing in marketing is to attract new customers while at the same time, keeping your most valuable clients.

To accomplish this feat, you must devise and implement a strategy that builds, fosters, nurtures and extends relationships with your customers.

Your brick and mortar business profits when the earnings from retained customers exceed the costs to acquire and to service customers over time.

That's it, end of story.

And while we're at it, advertising is just one aspect of marketing.

Marketing isn't advertising.

It can be a tactic you use, but when the sun goes down at the end of the day, advertising should be just one part of your total marketing strategy.

Marketing, in a traditional sense, is the overall umbrella that includes advertising, promotion, publicity, and public relations.

The classic example of marketing can be found in a "Readers Digest" quote in the article, "Promoting Issues and Ideas" by M. Booth and Associates, Inc.

> "... if the circus is coming to town and you paint a sign saying 'Circus Coming to the Fairground Saturday,' that's advertising.

If you put the sign on the back of an elephant and walk it into town, that's promotion.

If the elephant walks through the mayor's flower bed, that's publicity.

And if you get the mayor to laugh about it, that's public relations.

If the town's citizens go the circus, you show them the many entertainment booths, explain how much fun they'll have spending money at the booths, answer their questions and ultimately, they spend a lot at the circus; that's sales."

***

As with many points that we touch on in this book, we could spend a considerable amount of time talking about each aspect of marketing, publicity, sales and so on.

You could devote countless hours studying a litany of New York *Times* best-selling marketing books from the greatest minds on the subject.

With your newfound knowledge, you could spend your time, effort and resources pursuing every nuance available to you for each marketing endeavor.

You could, but should you?

Remember it's very easy to make a subject complex with a whole dictionary full of unique terms and particular theories.

Honestly, that's how you sell books and get lucrative speaking engagements—but it's much harder to make something simple that works.

That's why we spent two years designing and testing the entire A.I.M. program so you could set up the whole program in less than a day.

Straightforward and results-driven programs work best.

The marketing definition we just gave you works every time for brick and mortar businesses.

Write it down and make it your mantra when considering your future marketing options.

While we're on a roll, let's debunk another common misconception right now.

Are Sales the Goal of Advertising?

Too many small business owners believe the ultimate purpose of their marketing efforts is sales.

Sadly, this couldn't be further from the truth.

Sales are secondary to your marketing efforts.

A vast majority of small business owners we talk to think sales is the top goal.

When we ask them, "How was your last advertising promotion?" most will turn to their computer and look up sales numbers for the period in question.

If sales were good, the campaign worked.

If sales were weak, the campaign didn't work.

Clearly, that notion doesn't paint the entire picture because it doesn't address the issue of your merchandising, incoming foot traffic, or the ability of your sales staff to convert.

To look at just the sales results as a barometer of a campaign's success is far too simplistic.

In reality, you could have a great ad campaign that drives qualified leads to your business but fails miserably because of your weak sales team, your lackluster merchandise selection, or something outside of your control such as the weather or unexpected drop in the economy. None of those conversion failures would be the fault of the campaign.

Okay, now that we have a common understanding of what marketing is and isn't, let's move into the challenges your brick and mortar store is facing right now in measuring the effectiveness of your current marketing.

Why Measuring the Success of Marketing Programs Is Hard

It's easy to ask the question, "What kind of results does my marketing programs deliver?"

The cold, hard reality is that finding the answers can be tough and requires patience.

It could be months before you know if most campaigns are profitable. Unfortunately, in today's world, most small businesses only consider the short term results.

So before we move forward, let's take a moment and talk about this most "Holy Grail" of ubiquitous business buzzwords, ROI, or as it refers to this point, the Return On Marketing Investment (ROMI).

Today everybody wants the bottom line on marketing's contribution to business goals, and ROMI is the handy yardstick they reach for most often.

As a bit of trivia, ROI's business roots are actually in evaluating one-time capital projects.

So that begs the question, "Is marketing a one-time capital project?"

Clearly, it is not.

The question quickly comes down to this, is "Return On Marketing Investment" an accurate way to measure marketing effectiveness?

Sadly, and perhaps even shockingly to some, the answer is no—and here's why.

It's not that the notion of ROMI is evil or anything.

After all, linking marketing to financial performance is critical.

It's just that many small business owners who use ROMI aren't applying it correctly, or they mean something else.

Worse yet, they are usually trying to measure the wrong metric for the results they need.

So they end up spending money on the wrong objective, customer target, or touch point, all the while thinking they are doing the right thing.

Few Small Businesses Measure ROMI the Same

When we ask ten small business owners how they calculate the ROMI of their overall marketing strategy, we normally get ten different, often convoluted answers—especially if we dig a little bit into their methodology.

When you ask those same business owners how they calculate the ROMI of their marketing, they usually say something like this, "I spend a certain percentage of the store's profits a year on marketing."

Sometimes they will say, "If I spend money on advertising and sales go up, then I spend more money on the same kind of advertising."

The hard truth is that some small business owners have only a vague, shadowy notion of the return on their marketing investment and therein lies the problem.

If you don't have specific, predetermined goals for your marketing and don't have a reliable means to measure your results, then you will always be flying blind.

How will you know what works and what doesn't?

In today's tough economic climate can you afford to waste money on marketing that doesn't work?

You'll probably end up doing what so many small business owners do when they're frustrated with their lack of marketing success.

They just dump their advertising budget into print and cross their fingers that it will work better than it did the last time.

So where does that leave us?

As always, exactly where we need to be!

Align Your Metrics with Your Marketing Goals

We want a metric that aligns, supports, and gauges the success of our stated marketing objectives of attracting and retaining profitable customers for your business.

The metric that Four Grainer has developed is known as A.C.T., which is an acronym for "Acquired Customer Traffic."

A.C.T. represents the price you pay to acquire a full range of traffic through your front door.

As always, it is up to you and your team to convert this full range of traffic into buying clients.

Let's go back to our definition of marketing.

"Marketing is about attracting and retaining profitable customers to your business."

Not so surprisingly, the A.I.M. program has those same goals because it drives the full range of client traffic into your store.

In its simplest form, it can be worked out by this formula:

Divide the total costs associated with increasing foot traffic to your store by the total number of people who came into your store, within a particular time frame.

A good example would be if you spent $1,000 on a magazine ad last month and ten people came into your store because of that ad, then your cost to acquire that traffic is $100. $1,000 divided by 10 equals $100.

The most important key metric to track when measuring the effectiveness of your marketing campaigns is the cost to drive traffic into your store.

This simple statistic will help you evaluate the overall rate of growth of your business.

If the cost to find and convert people to purchasing clients is too high, your business won't be viable in the long-term.

The A.C.T. number is a very handy tool to evaluate each of your ongoing marketing efforts against each other as well.

With this tool, you can quickly compare apples to apples in your marketing portfolio and determine which of your marketing efforts are making the grade, and which ones are falling short.

You're suddenly free from John Wanamaker's famous advertising dilemma—"Half the money I spend on advertising is wasted; the trouble is I don't know which half"—because you will know.

How Your "Actively Involved Marketing" Program Solves This Problem

So we now know the difficulties you face in measuring the effectiveness of your marketing programs.

We're aware that increasing the full range of traffic to your store is vital for the survival and growth of your business.

Now let's show you how quickly your A.I.M. program solves these problems for you.

The genuine beauty of the program lies in its simplicity.

Want to measure how many people are driven to your store come in to sign the Community Outreach Program?

How do you know if they're new to your brick and mortar location?

Just ask them as they are signing up, "Is this your first time visiting our store?"

Remember the block on the signup form that supporters fill out under the particular charity's tab?"

The "Yrs: ___" block is an excellent way to start this conversation because they will ask you what it means.

If five people have "0" in the "Yrs: ___" block out of 20 who signed up, then you know for certain the "Actively Involved Marketing" (A.I.M.) program has given your store a 25% increase in new people through the door.

Just that easy!

What's not easy for many small businesses is how to measure the effectiveness of their marketing efforts.

Let's see if the A.I.M. program can help your business here by taking a look at the challenges you're facing.

Four Challenges to Measuring Marketing Programs

You have to know when to measure

The money you invest today in marketing will have an uncertain impact at an unknown point in the future.

Last month's trade show or merchandise presentation may deliver results next month, or perhaps not for two years, but marketers need to decide where to invest their budget today.

The type of product you are selling is also an important factor to consider.

A newly released album or a new diet product may produce instant results from your marketing campaign, where more complex products such as cars, boats, and industrial sales may require relatively lengthy campaigns.

Multiple touches

Proverbial marketing wisdom says at least seven different client interactions are needed to convert a cold lead into a sale.

Whether or not this is the correct number, the principle conveys an element of truth: every marketer knows it takes multiple touches to create a customer.

This fact makes it difficult to allocate revenue to any single contact.

Multiple influencers

Your marketing has to influence not only the potential client but those who impact that potential customer.

Now that word of mouth recommendations and criticisms spread through social media faster than fire in a dry field, influencers are the people your customers follow on social media, blogs, and anyone they trust for advice.

Always remember that influencers drive action, not just awareness.

As an example, perhaps you're considering buying a car.

How many people do you talk to before you make the purchase?

Those people you seek advice from are influencers of the outcome, and a car manufacturer's brand message has to resonate in a positive way with them, so they will endorse the goods and services when asked.

Different marketing programs affect each person differently, so it is a challenge to know which programs have the most impact.

Extraneous variables

In many cases, factors outside of the sphere of marketing's control can significantly affect program results—from macroeconomic trends, to the weather, the quality of your sales team, to news breaking world events.

If revenues increased because the economy improved, can you claim your marketing programs delivered a better ROI?

The Four Grainer A.I.M. Program Answers These Questions

Point One: When to measure?

You can evaluate the effectiveness of the program on a daily basis just by counting how many people signed the book and if they purchased something that day.

In fact, if you diligently searched each month, you will find that a large percentage of those who signed the book came back to make a purchase within a year.

Point Two: Multiple touches?

For 20% to 35% of the people, the initial contact with the store will be when they sign the book for their charity.

Sending a follow-up email the next day thanking them for coming in could be the second touch.

From there the sky is the absolute limit.

Each person is added to your mailing list when they sign the book.

Gone are the days of buying a list, because you are going to grow your own organically, and you're going to fill it with people who have a genuine interest in your business.

This one point alone could be worth the price of the entire program if you're skilled at generating business from your list.

One of the favorite mantras of marketing professionals is, "The gold is in the list."

Point Three: Multiple Influencers

There is a dynamic synergy that takes place in a charitable organization as they rally around the common cause of coming in to sign the book.

In so many positive ways, those who have already signed influence others to come in.

Email blasts, text messaging, phone calls, Instagram postings of them signing, Facebook posts and many others examples are providing multiple points of influence to the group.

Consider this one example.

A charity who rallies 25 people to come to your store to sign the book typically has five to ten times that many people on just their email list alone, not counting their much larger mailing list.

Our #1 question to every chairperson who was picking up the donation at the end was, "What did you do to energize your base to sign the book?"

We've found that for a charity to motivate 25 people to come into the store to sign, they've sent out three or four email blasts alone, not counting talking about it at meetings, text blasts, and social media interactions.

If you took into account just one charity's total email list, we are talking hundreds, if not thousands of emails, contacts, and touch points.

All of these touches are touting the virtues and generosity of your business towards the local community.

Think seriously about that one aspect of this program.

Let it marinate in your consciousness for a moment.

The truth is, you couldn't buy that much positive goodwill, that much free advertisement and word of mouth publicity.

Want to blow your mind?

Take the hundreds, to thousands of helpful contacts for your store generated by just one charity, and now multiply it by 20 charitable organizations.

Now it gets interesting because the total number of supportive contacts for all of the charitable organizations combined can create for your location jumps into the tens of thousands quickly.

The A.I.M. program is a marketer's dream come true!

Point Four: Extraneous variables.

Unfortunately, you will always have charitable needs in your local community.

It will always be constant, so will people seeking local businesses' support to battle those needs.

The economy may fluctuate up and down, but those companies that can drive clients into their store on demand will always have the advantage.

Business a little tight right now?

Contact three of the larger non-profit 501(c)3 charities in your area and explain your Community Outreach Program.

Invite them to participate with a 30-day signup window.

They send in 25 to 100 people each, which for three charities would be 75 to 300 extra people coming in your store for the 30 days.

Now it's up to your sales team to convert them to buyers and long-term clients of the location.

From experience, you will know what percentage of those who sign the book will make a purchase within 30 days and on average the dollars generated.

With three telephone calls you've gotten your business back on track, supported your local community, and had thousands of enthusiastic contacts.

Time for a rhetorical question.

"What small business owner wouldn't make those three calls?"

Hope that whets your appetite to delve in deeper to the A.I.M. program.

We know you probably have more questions now than before.

You're Ready to Move On

So now you've got your physical binder ready.

You've completed all of the needed forms for the program.

We've gotten a grip on our standard marketing definition; as well as, insight into how we're going to measure the results.

The next question we have to address is the one that many of you have probably been wondering about for the past couple of chapters.

"How much do we give the charity per person that signs the Community Outreach Program book under their particular tab?"

Let's get that one answered right now because we believe in these words of wisdom first spoken in 1562, by John Trusler:

"No time like the present, a thousand unforeseen circumstances may interrupt you in the future."

Chapter Nine

HOW MUCH DO YOU DONATE PER PERSON?

*"Advertising is totally unnecessary unless
you hope to make money"*
—Jef I. Richards

W E THOROUGHLY UNDERSTAND THE challenges in setting up a new program, even one as easy and as intuitive as the A.I.M. program.

For most brick and mortar businesses, the most challenging part of this entire book is figuring out how much to give the charity for each person that comes in.

The best place to start the search for that elusive number is by taking a look at what you are currently spending to drive traffic to your front door.

In the case of our test store, it was a good reason to take a microscope to their entire marketing program, and maybe that's the case for you as well.

We analyzed the following parameters:

- Store's overall margin.
- Stock turn rate.

- Natural organic traffic flows based on data from their front door's traffic counter system.
- How often the average client purchased from the store.
- Average price point per purchase.
- The estimated customer lifetime value. (CLV)
- Sales closing ratio per sales associate and for the store as a whole.
- Every touchpoint with the client. (print, radio, tv, newspaper, magazines, etc.)
- Previous charitable donation amounts and how effective they were at driving traffic.
- Marketing budget available.
- Overall client growth and retention strategy.

In fact, we spent several days formulating the top business models when it comes to customer acquisition, retention, projected costs and estimated bottom line profit over a three-year span adjusted for inflation.

We had neatly laser printed pages filled with various formulas, stats, and every number we could throw at this one simple question.

Not to be outdone, we had beautiful multi-colored pie charts, slides and impressive graphics to tell our story in glorious Technicolor.

You name it, and we had it in duplicate, triplicate, bound and ready to go.

Guess what we learned at the end of it all?

Don't over think this one number for two simple reasons:

- The goal of the entire program is to ensure enough of an incentive for the charity to act.
- You can always change the number up or down for the next charity.

In case you were wondering, yes, we did get it down to a single number, but it was a series of formulas that only those who were math majors in college would love.

Something else that we found out was that raising the amount per person who signed the book, didn't always determine how many supporters of that charity would come through our front door.

The truth we learned was that some charities were just more organized than others, their followers more energized.

Some of the small charitable organizations had a passionate base that was willing to drive to the store to sign up, while surprisingly some of the best known national charities had few that bothered to come in.

In many cases we could've offered the moon and all of the stars as an incentive, but for some charities that wouldn't have changed the number who eventually signed up one bit.

Keep that fact in mind as you determine the amount per person that you feel comfortable with donating.

A good point to remember when you're determining your total donation amount is the projected number of supporters a charity can bring into your store.

While almost every charitable organization that signs up will tell you, they can easily deliver 20, 50, 100 or more supporters to sign the Community Outreach Program book under the particular charity's tab.

The truth is they can't.

For two solid years, we tested the program in a store with a stellar reputation of serving the local community.

The test store has been in business for 20 years with excellent name recognition, a well-deserved reputation for quality, service and unwavering commitment to the community.

The store sits in a medium sized town with impressive demographics.

All of the leading demographic indicators are there from exceptional school quality to impressive household incomes, education level, disposable income, house size and a genuine sense of community spirit.

This planned community is one of the most livable cities in the state by all measurements and surveys.

Seriously, this area is a marketer's dream come true.

We say all of that to say this.

Our test store was sitting in the perfect environment for this program to drive in the maximum number of supporters, yet the results were not budget-busting.

Don't lose sleep over the amount you're giving per person just yet.

We're going to pull back the curtain and show you the actual results from our brick and mortar store over the two years.

Let's start with the first year.

First Year Actual Expense / Revenue Results

211 people came in to sign the Community Outreach Program book.

11 local charities in total signed up.

Three of those charities had zero participation from their supporters.

Of the top two traffic-driving 501(c)3s, one charity had 93 sign up, the other had 62, the other six averaged 9.33 people who came in to sign.

The store gave merchandise/gift certificates for goods and services totaling $9,500 at retail value to the eight charities.

In total, the store generated $4,100 retail in new sales from supporters the day they signed the book.

Within a week of signing the book, those who signed came back to purchase $6,250 in goods and services.

Thus the store generated $10,350 in total sales if you combine same day purchases and those who made a purchase within a week of signing the book.

Let's compare the $10,350 in retail sales to an expense of $9,500 in retail goods and services.

The margin rate for the store is 50%, thus the $10,350 in retail sales produced $5,175 in gross profit.

The $9,500 in donations and gift certificates also has a margin rate of 50% which brings the actual cost down to $4,750.

The net result of the first year showed a bottom increase of $425 for running the program.

($4,750 in expenses minus $5,175 in gross profit) to bring in 211 people through the door.

Before we move on to the second year results, let's determine the Acquired Customer Traffic (A.C.T.) of the first year.

As a way of reminder, here is the formula for A.C.T.

Divide the total costs associated with increasing foot traffic to your store by the total number of people who came into your store, within a particular period.

Now that we have the formula let's plug in the numbers.

Usually, we would plug in the cost of the program; however, the first year the store made money to the tune of $425.

We divide the positive $425 by the 211 people who came into the location.

The result shows the store made $2.01 per person that signed the charity book.

This point alone is why you never donate cash to a charity.

You need the margin provided by your goods and services to offset the expenses.

Just as a disclaimer at this point.

Your results will vary, obviously, but you also have to admit, it's great when your marketing is 100% verifiable and makes you money.

Granted, those are strong first year numbers, but the great news doesn't stop there.

The client breakdown is in many ways, even more exciting!

First Year Actual Client Breakdown

Point One—Of the 211 who signed the book, 72 people had never been in the store before.

That is a staggering 34%!

If you considered just this one factor alone, if the entire marketing program only generated this one positive result than it would be a resounding success.

Point Two—Of the 211 who signed the book, 116 people / 59.7% of the total had not been in the store within the past year, many hadn't been in there for several years.

We cannot tell you how important this portion of your client base is to your future business because you get to ask the easy follow-up question, "What's kept you away for so long?"

Their answers can provide a treasure trove of vital information for your business.

This unique window into the client's perceptions and views will sometimes shock you, other times will sadden you, but will always give you the brutal answers you desperately need to hear if you are going to make your business a better place to shop.

The staff got the opportunity to ask these three fundamental marketing questions.

- "Why haven't you come into the store before?"
- "Why did you stop shopping with us?"
- "What keeps you coming back to our store?"

Those are the three "deep data mining" questions that major corporations today are spending millions of dollars on to figure out electronically and you get it first hand from your clients as a bonus!

To top it all off, you get the answers face to face, and you have the chance to ask follow-up questions as well.

If A.I.M. only provided this information to you, it would be your most valuable form of marketing.

Why?

Your traditional media (print, radio, television, email blasts, mail) is only one-way communication or what we refer to as outbound marketing.

Your company initiates the conversation and sends its message out to an audience.

In A.I.M. you have the face to face opportunity for a meaningful dialogue with your clients.

It gives you the information you need to sincerely make your marketing, your product selection, and every other part of your business better right now!

Point Three—Of the 211 who signed the book, 23 people / 10.9% of the total had been in the store within the past year.

Our original pre-conceived notion was that the majority of individuals who signed the book would be those who were the most familiar with the store and that just wasn't the case.

We thought because they knew where the store was located and had a recent history of interacting with the staff, that it would lower the barrier to entry to come in to sign the book.

Honestly, we were excited to be wrong, because it demonstrated the real power of local charities.

The results show that even if someone had an unfavorable experience with the store in the past, they still came in to sign the book because of their devotion to the charity.

Therein lies a real example of the power of local charities to move their supporters to action and the cornerstone of why this program works.

Let's stop here for a moment to state the obvious, but relevant facts.

The A.I.M. program is the first marketing program that allows the small business owner to track and verify every aspect of the program. As you can see, there are no complicated formulas, no need to take someone else's word or believe their voodoo math on some obscure aspect of it.

You are in total control every step of the way.

In many cases, you are the one who gets a chance to talk to the clients and witness the results first hand.

You also control the profitability.

Five Points to Control Profitability

Point One: Your sales team's ability to convert the traffic.

The better your team is at selling those who walk through the door, the greater your profit, thus reducing overall expenses (i.e. Apple, Verizon, Battery Plus).

Point Two: The price point of your store's merchandise selection.

Modestly priced items mean you will have to sell more items to generate the profit dollars you need to keep the expense low (i.e. Dillard's, Macy's, Belk).

Point Three: Your merchandise markup structure.

Lower margins dictate you will have to sell a greater number of units to pull in the profit dollars you need to lower the expense structure (i.e. Costco, Dollar Store, Wal-Mart).

Point Four: How much you budget for generating traffic through your door.

There are volumes written on this topic alone with opinions running the full gamut of formulas and theories.

For this program, set a number you're comfortable with knowing you can adjust it for the next charity.

Point Five: How long you run the program each year.

If you operate the program for nine months of the year, it will cost you more undoubtedly than if you shorten the window to four months.

The control is in your hands.

Second Year Actual Expense / Revenue Results

521 people came in to sign the Community Outreach Program book under their particular charity's tab.

Organically, through word of mouth endorsements, the message has spread around the local community.

21 charitable organizations signed up the second year

Three charities had zero participation.

We made the program available for the same amount of time both years.

Of the two largest 501(c)3s, one had 95 sign up, and the other 63.

The other 16 charities averaged 29 people per charity.

The 18 charities received $16,500 at full retail in merchandise/gift certificates.

In total, the store generated $6,600 retail value in new sales from supporters the day they signed the book.

Within a week of signing the book for their charity, those who signed purchased $8,750 retail in goods and services.

Combining same day purchases and those made within a week of signing the book resulted in income of $15,350 at retail for the second year.

The margin rate for the store is 50%, thus the $15,350 in retail sales generated the second-year produced $7,675 in gross profit.

The merchandise and gift certificates donated totaled $16,500 at retail value, thus with a 50% margin, our bottom line expense for the donation falls to $8,250.

Just to be crystal clear, we have to say this again.

This point is why you never donate cash to a charity.

Your merchandise has margin built into it which always lowers your expenses from the face value of the donation.

What about the cost of "Acquired Client Traffic," you ask?

Let's plug in the figures.

Our second-year total expense was ($8,250 in donations minus $7,675 in gross profit) $575.

We take the total second-year total cost of $575 divided by the 521 clients the program drove into the store shows an "Acquired Customer Traffic" (A.C.T.) cost of $1.10 per person who signed the book.

This result begs the natural question, "How does $1.10 per person relate to this store's other marketing efforts?"

We could answer that question, and even though we live in a "Wikileaks" kind of world right now, we aren't going to divulge that information.

For the sake of discussion, let's spin the question around and ask, "How does $1.10 per person expense relate to YOUR marketing efforts?"

Our first guess is that $1.10 wins against your best marketing A.C.T. number.

Our second guess is that in most cases, $1.10 per person expense to drive people into your store wins by a tsunami-sized amount.

Our third and final guess would be that most small businesses if they are honest with themselves, have no way to measure the effectiveness of their marketing efforts accurately.

Are we right on all counts?

Second Year Actual Client Breakdown

Point One—Of the 521 who signed the book, 193 people / 37% of the total had never been in the store before.

Compare those results with the 72 new people / 34% of the total of the first year.

Point Two—Of the 521 who signed the book, 226 people / 44% had not been in the store within the past year.

Compared to 116 people / 59.7% for the previous year.

Point Three—Of the 521 who signed the book, 102 people / 29% of the total had been in the store within the past year.

That compares to the previous year results of 23 people / 10.9% of the total.

While the percentages shifted among the three categories each year, the trend line, as you can see, is starting to firm up.

Clearly, there is a substantial portion of the full range of people the program is driving into the store that has never stepped foot into this brick and mortar location, as well as, a substantial portion that hasn't been back for at least a year.

Year One Vs. Year Two Results

Total traffic through the door: 211 vs. 521. 60% increase over the 1st year.

The number of charities who signed up: 11 vs. 21. 91% increase over the first year.

Sales generated the day they signed: $4,100 vs. $6,600. 61% increase over the 1st year.

Sales generated the first week after signing: $6,250 vs. $8,750. 40% increase over the 1st year.

Total purchased the first week at full retail: $10,350 vs. $15,350. 48% increase over the 1st year generated sales.

Total donation expense at full retail: $9,500 vs. $16,500. 74% increase over the 1st year.

Acquired Client Traffic amount: A positive $2.01 vs. an expense of $1.10 per person who signed the book.

Combined Two Year Results—Wrap Up

Over the two years, 265 people who had never been into the store before, got a chance to hear the brand message first hand and experience what the store had to offer for themselves.

342 people hadn't been to the business for at least a year, and for most, it had been many years, came back in to become reacquainted with the team and the new merchandise.

125 were those whose face probably looked familiar because they had visited the store within the year.

The good news is that for these 125 clients, they see you, and what the store represents to the community, in an entirely different light.

No longer is your business just a place to shop, but now they get a chance to see it as a business that gives back to their community.

In many ways, it validated their recent purchase and confirmed their instincts to trust your business.

All told, 732 people came through the door to sign under their favorite charity's tab for the two years.

SIGNIFICANT The program was run for nine months each year.

We blocked off November, December, and January each of the years, so for the two years, the program ran just 18 months in total.

The reason for the time blocked off was to concentrate on the profitable seasonal business, and to reduce the number of days the program was available to charities, and thus reduce the operating expense.

The only advertising to support the program was to place a Community Outreach Program tab on the business's website.

Truly this was old fashion word of mouth advertising, and it quickly spread among the various charitable organizations.

Over the two years, 32 charities signed up costing the store $25,000 retail which was lessened by the generated total revenue of $22,700 retail.

The margin rate for the store is 50%, thus the $22,700 in retail sales produced $11,350 in gross profit.

The m erchandise a nd g ift c ertificates do nated to taled $25,000 at retail value, thus with a 50% margin, our bottom line cost for the donation falls to $12,500.

The net result was an expense to the store ($12,500 cost minus $11,350 income at cost) for $1,150 to get 732 people into their store during the two years.

With regards to the total Acquired Customer Traffic (A.C.T.) number, it would be $1,150 divided by 732 which results in a cost of $1.57.

After running the program for two years, the A.I.M. program brought in 732 people to their store at the cost of $1.57 per person.

So now that we've pulled back the curtain and shown you the great and powerful Oz, what does that do for you?

Does it help determine your business's price per client offer to your local charities? We hope it does, but here is something else to consider that we've found out.

The price per person for the first 25 should be different that the amount per person after the charity has surpassed that milestone.

Let's go back to our printed example to explain.

Here are the five levels we used:

Bronze Level—Receive a $100 gift certificate by having five people sign under your charity's tab in our store.

Silver Level—Receive a $250 gift certificate by having 6 to 10 people sign under your tab.

Gold Level—Receive a $500 gift certificate by having 11 to 15 people sign under your tab.

Platinum Level—Receive a $750 gift certificate by having 16 to 20 people sign under your tab.

Diamond Level—Receive a $1,000 gift certificate by having 21 to 25 people sign under your tab.

*** The good news is that we continue to increase your donation for every supporter you have over the Diamond Level!

The reason to publish the first five levels is to energize the charities for immediate action.

If the potential reward for getting 25 supporters to come into the store is too small, most charities won't put much emphasis on motivating their followers. If the potential reward for the first 25 supporters is too high, the expense to the store will be too great.

We've shown you all of the results from the test store as a guide; however, it comes down to how your individual store is set up.

Your particular business model, expense structure, and margin goals determine your final cost per person through the door.

No two independent brick and mortar stores have the same cost structure or profit margin.

What we do know is that you will probably have to do some adjusting of the price per person for the first 25 in the beginning.

Once you start to see the results, start to see charities eagerly signing up, you know that you've found a good number to stimulate them to action.

At that point, you just need to see if it fits into your business model on a long-term basis.

As we mentioned earlier, the Community Outreach Program has to be a win/win for you and the charities.

***

Now let's tackle the price per person after the first 25 supporters have signed under the charity's tab in the Community Outreach Program book.

We found that if you maintain the same price per person all the way through the program, the program will be too expensive, and won't generate significantly more people through the door.

In essence, there is the "Law of Diminishing Returns" at work here which states, "The point at which the level of profits or benefits gained is less than the amount of money or energy invested."

In everyday speech, "Sometimes, the juice isn't worth the squeeze."

The reason that we don't publish the donation amount past the first five levels is twofold.

First: The vast majority of charities won't get past the 25 people sign up mark.

Second: To allow the business to determine on its own what is appropriate for a charitable organization that drives a large number of supporters into your business.

As part of the initial conversation with the charity, we always touch on these four points.

Point 1—We've posted the donation amount for the first 25 that sign under your charity's tab in the Community Outreach Program book, but we continue to give past that level.

Point 2—In fact, we don't have a top end to how much we donate to a charity. We just continue to give as you continue to bring people in.

Point 3—We want to give more, help us to give more by getting the word out. It's all based on you.

Point 4—We'll give you a hard copy of the sign-up sheets at the end so you know exactly who came in to support your charity.

If they persist on asking how much your business is willing to donate for a certain number of signatures, just give them these three sentences.

- "Our goal is to give as much as we can to our local charities, that's why we developed the Community Outreach Program."
- "Honestly, we'd love to see you bring in hundreds of supporters to sign the book."
- "We always take a look at the end of the sign-up period to see how many people came in to support the charity and donate accordingly."

A politician's answer to the question?

Yes, but the thing is, you don't want to be pressured to give a specific dollar amount per person.

Remember it is all about both the charity and the business benefiting from this transaction.

The cost per person for the first 25 should be higher than the 26th through the 100th person who signs up because it entices more charities into action.

Local 501(c)3 organizations will look at the first five levels and determine in a few seconds whether it is worth it for them to sign up.

As you're figuring out the number for the first 25 and the other number for the 26th and beyond sign up, remember all the fringe benefits we've outlined from this program that you are going to receive.

Make it worth their while, but don't break the bank.

While we're at it, some charities—in fact, some big name charities—will sign up for the program and not have a single person come to sign the book.

Embarrassing to be sure for the charity, but don't feel pressured to give them something regardless.

It's our personal belief that if a 501(c)3 charitable organization can't manage to have four people come and sign the Community Outreach Program book they haven't upheld their part of the bargain, and thus deserve nothing from us.

When asked if we still wanted to donate to their cause the response was.

- "We want to support as many charities as we can in our local community."

- "We've developed this Community Outreach Program to provide a fair, equitable way to support every 501(c) 3 charity that applies regardless of size."

- "While the results were not what either of us had hoped for, let's put our heads together next year to find out how we can get people in the store to sign under your charity."

More politician speak?

Yes, but the good news here is that it's rare that a charity can't get five supporters through the door.

Let's be serious for a moment.

Can't they get five people to come in?

Where is the person who filled out the form and where are the officers of the charity? If they don't care enough, then why should you?

This program has to be a win/win for both your business and the charity.

**SIGNIFICANT* While we're talking about the expense side of the program, there is a little-known caveat that you should be aware of now.

Not all gift certificates get redeemed.

In fact, during the two years of our test, a full 17% of the gift certificates did not get redeemed.

We could debate whether unredeemed gift certificates are positive because they lower the cost of the program, or if they are negative because they don't give the store the opportunity to upsell the client.

The truth is the lower valued gift certificates are more likely not to be redeemed than the higher valued ones. Of course, that makes sense, but in the end, you can't control if the gift certificates get redeemed or not, or know why some never do.

All you can focus on is providing the opportunity to support the local charity in their efforts and, in return, growing your business. The expenses we listed during the two-year test were with redeemed and unredeemed gift certificates counted as an expense.

We did that because the redeemed ones are an actual expense, but the unredeemed gift certificates represent a potential, future expense.

Only time will tell if some of the 17% non-redeemed get redeemed.

Our experience would lead us to believe that there will be around 10% to 15% of the gift certificates that will never be redeemed.

Just thought you should take that caveat into consideration when you are figuring out your potential expenses for the program.

Wrapping Up the Financial End

We hope that after looking at the actual results from running the program for two years in a brick and mortar store that you are more comfortable with setting up your particular A.I.M. expense structure.

We wish we could have given you one universal number for the first 25 signups and another for the 26th through 100, but it just isn't possible without knowing your business.

What you're going to find is that it will involve a gut feeling based on our results, and a bit of trial and error tailored to your store's business model.

Don't lose sleep over those two numbers, pick them, and modify them from year to year.

The point that we are positive about is that it legitimately works on several financial and emotional levels at once.

In 25+ years, we've never seen a marketing program that was as interactive and downright fun as the A.I.M. program.

Always a smile, always heart-warming, fun, and never, ever dull.

Yes, the financial results were there at every level, but seeing the smile spread across a store associate's face as they reached for the book to give to a charity's supporter was worth something as well.

Last Chapter Wrap-Up

In our last and final chapter, we ease your concerns about launching the program by sharing the exact roleplaying training outline we used to unveil the program.

As you know by now, we love quotes.

Here's one that's appropriate.

"A journey of a thousand miles starts with a single step, and if that step is the right one, it becomes the last step." Quote from Laozi, an ancient Chinese philosopher, writer, and the founder of philosophical Taoism.

We now have the last step to make on our journey together.

Chapter Ten

FEARS, TEARS, & LAUNCHING THE RIGHT WAY

"Stop being afraid of what could go wrong and start being positive about what could go right."
—*Zig Ziglar*

W E'RE PROUD OF YOU!
You've made it through the book, and that in and of itself is an achievement.

The Pew Research Center reported that almost 25% of American adults have not read a single book in the past year.

When we say they haven't read a book we mean, they hadn't cracked a paperback, fired up a Kindle, or even hit play on an audiobook while in the car.

In fact, the number of non-book-readers has nearly tripled since 1978.

You're an exception because you're driven to succeed.

For you knowledge is power.

We firmly believe you now have in your hands a proven new way of getting results from your marketing.

Finally, you can see how embracing the needs of your local charities can drive additional traffic and sales to your business.

Now all that's left is getting the program off the ground.

Launching the Program the Right Way

Whenever you consider introducing something new, there is always a bit of fear and trepidation.

It's only natural.

To abate some of those fears (and potential tears), we've added the role play training outline we used to train the staff when we first rolled out the program.

The conversations are grouped into the three categories to make it easier for you.

- Management to Charity Partner.
- Management to Staff.
- Staff to Charity Supporters.

First up, let's take a look at the typical discussion the charity partners have with the store manager concerning the Community Outreach Program.

Management to Charity Partner

CHARITY: Hi, we're from ABC charity, and we were wondering if you would like to donate to our big fund-raiser event?

MGMT: We'd be thrilled to participate. In fact, have you heard about our Community Outreach Program?

If you're a 501(c)3 charitable organization, your donation amount is based solely on your efforts.

The more supporters you get to come in and sign the Community Outreach Program book under your particular charity's tab, the more we donate to you!

To make it even better, you can choose between a gift certificate, merchandise, or break up the total amount and get both from our store.

CHARITY: Wow, that's great. What do we have to do?

MGMT: The first step would be to fill out this Charitable Partner sign up form, or fill it out online at our website and hit "Send.

The online version is located under the "Contact Us" portion of our online site.

We will contact you when we receive the form so we can review the information you've put down.

At that time, we'll confirm your exact start and ending dates.

This gives you a window of opportunity to rally your supporters to come in and sign the book under your particular charitable organization tab.

There is no obligation to purchase, in fact, all that we ask is they be over 18 years of age, and signup for only one charity per year.

At the end of the sign-up period, we'll let you know the final number of your supporters who came in.

We'll also talk about the amount of our donation and if you want merchandise, gift certificate, or both.

Also, we will give you a copy of all of the signup pages for your charity so you can see who to thank for taking the time to come in.

Please feel free to call anytime during the process to find out how many of your supporters have come in.

If you've any questions, we have a (F.A.Q.) online at our Community Outreach Program tab under the "Contact Us" section or give us a call.

In all honesty, the conversation to explain the program is just that quick and easy.

Let's take a moment to look at an example of how to give an overview of the program to your team members.

Management to Staff

Explaining the Community Outreach Program to your staff is just as easy.

STAFF: So what's the new marketing program?

MGMT: We're rolling out a new program that allows us to give back to our community for all the support they've given us over the years. It's called the Community Outreach Program, and it is easy to use.

At this point in the presentation to the staff, you walk them through the sign-up book, and the four stipulations on the actual sign-up form under the charity's tab:

- Must Be Over 18 Years Old To Sign Up
- Block Must Be Filled Out To Qualify
- Only Sign Up For One Charity Per Year
- You Will Be Added To Our Mailing List

The next part of the training includes the actual blocks of:

- Name
- Address
- Email Address
- Telephone Number
- Years since last visit _____

MGMT: So as you can see, this is straightforward in how they sign up, but two points might not be so obvious.

The first point is this is the first marketing program that we've used that drives measurable traffic to our front door.

Our goal is to connect with people in our community in a way that our ads in the magazines, on the radio, or on TV simply can't do.

With this program, we get the chance to meet one-on-one with current clients again, past customers, and those who have never been to our store.

The second point centers on the fact that this is the first marketing plan that owes its success or failure, in large part, to all of us on the team.

When they come through the door, we can either get to know them in a meaningful way or we can just show them where to provide the information we need and ignore them.

The choice is up to us, and that's why we say that the success of this marketing plan is in our hands.

If we take a little time to get to know them by asking questions like, "How did you get started supporting this charity?" or "What does your charity do for our community?

All of this will give us a chance to get to know them as people instead of just clients.

This is the best way to build your personal customer base because you're making the emotional connection first and that's a solid foundation for trust.

Perhaps the easiest way to start a conversation is by looking at the "Yrs: ____" section of the form.

If the number is zero, they've never shopped with us.

If it's another number it represents the number of years it's been since they've been into our store.

If they haven't been in before or haven't been in for years, offer to take them on a private guided tour.

Most people appreciate the individualized treatment.

Staff to Charity Supporters Roleplay

SUPPORTER: Hi, I'm here to sign the book for the ABC charity.

STAFF: Great, thanks for coming in.

Opening the Community Outreach Program binder to the ABC charity tab the team member says,

"Here's your charity's page and here's a pen."

As the individual fills out the required information of name, address, email address, telephone number and the "Yrs" line, the staff member says,

"The "Yrs" line is for how long since you've been in our store."

"If this is your first time in, then just put "0", if you've been in this year put "1.""

"If it has been longer than a year, then just put a number down for how many years since your last visit."

As the person is filling out the required information, the staff member says, "We're excited to be able to support local charities through this program."

"We're always looking for ways to give back to the community that has supported our business over these years."

After the individual had filled out the block, the staff member said, "Thanks for supporting the charity!"

"I see that you've put zero down on the "Yrs" line, does that mean you've never been to our store?"

SUPPORTER: I've never been here before.

STAFF: You haven't? Oh my gosh, well let me be the first to say welcome!

"If you've got a moment, let me give you a quick guided tour and introduce you to some of the great team members."

When the "Yrs" line was a "1", one of the store associate says, "So I see you've been in the store within a year, thank you for shopping with us!"

"If you don't mind me asking, did we get everything you needed that day, or are there any questions I could answer for you?"

If the client doesn't have any concerns, the staff member would say, "We appreciate you shopping with us and giving us this chance to support your charity.

"My name is Cynthia, and if there are any questions you might have about our store or our selection, please feel free to call me."

SIGNIFICANT The program was not designed to be a hook to get people through the door so that you could browbeat them or make them feel guilty about walking out the door without making a purchase.

This program isn't a stereotypical "Timeshare Condo" presentation.

You know the one where they give you a free weekend in a beautiful condo and all you have to do is sit through an hour long hardcore, elbow twisting presentation at the end of the week before you leave.

The goal here is to make a genuine business connection with the person.

Will you make sales that day because they came in to sign the book?

Yes, of course, you will, but that will happen naturally.

We're playing the long-game here because we want this program to produce a large number of clients for life, not a few scattered sales today because we shamed them into making a purchase.

When the "Yrs" line was "2" or greater we overheard a staff member say, "I couldn't help but notice that it has been years since you've visited our store."

"We've missed you, is there anything we can do to get you back?"

Another member of the staff took this opportunity to say, "So much has changed in the past years since you've been in, let me show you some of those changes."

The information that the staff members got from former clients was worth its weight in gold because it uncovered gaps in the product assortment, training opportunities, staff issues, and a myriad of other topics that the store would have never known about otherwise. In some ways, this kind of feedback itself was worth the effort.

***

Hope this helps you feel more comfortable in rolling out the "Actively Involved Marketing" (A.I.M.) program to your staff and the community.

Of course, you'll want to personalize the roleplaying questions and answers to fit your style.

Ultimately, they should serve as a solid foundation to build your presentation to your staff, charity volunteers, and the various charitable organizations that come knocking on your door.

So, through it all, here at the end, what have we learned?

The View Through the Rearview Mirror

Looking back over the development phase and the two years of running the program in a brick and mortar store, we've come to embrace our fears and doubts.

We know the status quo is persistent and resilient, especially in the way small businesses are feebly trying to get their message out.

The status quo exists because everyone wants it to.

So many believe that what they've got is probably better than the risk and fear that comes with change. That notion isn't new by any stretch.

The example that quickly comes to mind is Microsoft and their belief over a decade ago that their company was invincible.

They believed the insignificant search engines and Internet businesses in Silicon Valley couldn't possibly represent a threat.

In fact, Steve Ballmer, CEO of Microsoft, said, "Google's not a real company. It's a house of cards."

He also said, "There can't be any more deep technology in Facebook than what dozens of people could write in a couple of years; that's for sure."

Hindsight being what it is.

We would be willing to bet a large stack of folding money that Steve Ballmer wishes he had taken a more clean-sheet, "disruptive view" of the situation back then.

According to Forbes, Google is worth $560 billion.

What of that little business called Facebook?

According to Forbes, Facebook is worth a measly $350 billion.

Over and over, everyone is wrong—unless you believe innovation can change things.

It all starts with your belief that a clean-sheet disruptive approach to your marketing can produce the results your business needs now.

Start with supporting one of the 501(c)3 charities that darken your doorstep every week and see the results first hand.

From there you can make the decision to support more charitable organizations or stop the entire program.

At least you will have tried. At least you will know if it works for your particular business.

Our bet?

Once you've tried it, you'll wonder how your brick and mortar business ever survived without it.

One Last Thing

Can we ask a favor of you?

If you've gotten anything out of this book, we're hoping you'll do something for us.

Either give this copy to someone else or write a review in support of the book on Amazon.

Help us to spread the word to other small businesses that they don't have to live with their current marketing limitations.

Tell them you've found a better way.

You've given your customers a reason to chant your name!

WHAT'S UP NEXT?

Y OU'VE JUST FINISHED THE FIRST BOOK, "A Reason To Chant," which is a step by step guide on how to take control of your marketing to earn trust, devotion, and traffic to your brand forever.

Don't miss "Chant To Be Heard" which is the second of the three books in the "Chant For Business" series.

"Chant To Be Heard" supercharges the proven "Actively Involved Marketing" (A.I.M.) program, taking it to a whole new level!

Within this book, we show you how to energize your marketing to such a high level that others in the community are quite literally advertising for you every day.

We also walk you through the steps to easily take the information you've gathered in your Community Outreach binder and convert it from a name, address, telephone number, and email address to a purchasing client.

Each book in the series builds on the success and core concepts of the one before it.

The last book in the series is titled, "Power Chant For Success."

This book personally sherpas you to the lofty summit of the "Actively Involved Marketing" (A.I.M.) program.

From the summit, we guide you through the steps of how to expand your local market share substantially, extend your business reach well beyond your community, and develop a energized "brand evangelist" client base for life.

All three books were written by Rod Worley, the CEO of Four Grainer LLC and the host of "Inside the Jewelry Trade" Radio Show.

Four Grainer is a full range, results-driven jewelry industry exclusive consulting firm.

Our core mission is to solve our client's toughest challenges by providing unmatched services in strategy, consulting, digital marketing and operations.

At Four Grainer, we take an innovation-led approach to help our single and multi-unit clients "imagine and invent" their sustainable future today.

Since July of 2011, we have been delivering results and exceeding the expectations of our valued clients.

Contact us at FourGrainer.com if you have further questions, or simply want to talk about improving your business.